EMBRACING CONSCIOUS SIMPLICITY

Embracing Conscious Simplicity

through Awareness, Intention and Understanding

Barbara Bougher & Teresa Worthington

ISBN: 1530124360
ISBN 13: 9781530124367

*This book is for anyone who is seeking freedom
from all the inner and outer clutter that gets in the way
of the life they want to live.*

Kathie ~
May all that you
embrace bring you
joy and simplicity.
Thanks for your support ~
Barbara

CONTENTS

About the Authors

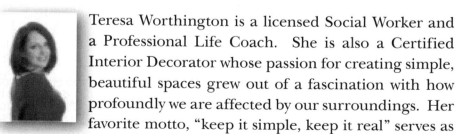

Barbara Bougher, ACC, is a Certified Organizer Coach and owner of Divine Order. She is grounded in the belief that we live from either a place of love or a place of fear and knows her authentic self is most evident from a place of love, understanding, and laughter. Barbara demonstrates caring optimism when coaching her clients to clear physical, mental, and emotional clutter, and experiences tremendous gratification when clients regain their power to make a difference in their lives.

Barbara lives in Carmel, Indiana where she enjoys her grown son and step-children and their wonderful families. She is grateful for her partner, Ed, who has made a difference in her life. Barbara can be reached through her website at www. DivineOrderForLife.com.

Teresa Worthington is a licensed Social Worker and a Professional Life Coach. She is also a Certified Interior Decorator whose passion for creating simple, beautiful spaces grew out of a fascination with how profoundly we are affected by our surroundings. Her favorite motto, "keep it simple, keep it real" serves as her reminder to strive for authenticity in life. She believes very strongly that staying conscious of what we choose to surround our self with, both physically and energetically, is key to living an empowered life.

Teresa lives outside of Lansing, Michigan with her husband, Dave and has two wonderful, grown sons, Tommy and Kenny, as well as one amazing stepson, Jay. All of who she counts among her blessings. She can be reached through her website at www.IntuitiveRedesigns.com.

INTRODUCTION

*"There is great freedom in simplicity of living. It is those
who have enough but not too much who are the happiest."*

~ PEACE PILGRIM

EMBRACING CONSCIOUS SIMPLICITY is about recognizing both the physical and non-physical clutter that distracts us from living our best life, and it is about empowering our self to make conscious choices about what we want to keep and what we want to let go. Indeed, there are many ways that we clutter up our life. While our physical clutter is the most recognizable, it is also often a frequent indicator that we have other types of clutter going on in our life too.

What we have both come to know in the course of our work is that often many of us are not consciously aware of how profoundly our physical spaces and our possessions impact and intertwine with every other aspect of our life, including our energy, our happiness, our finances, our health, our success, and our relationships. It is for these reasons we chose to create a book that is about much more than our physical belongings. It's about our self-awareness. It's about living a life that fully expresses who we are and promotes our happiness. It's about making conscious choices that empower us and support our dreams, and it's about making room in our everyday life for the things, people and activities we genuinely enjoy and value.

Only you can know what it means for you to live in conscious simplicity. Your version will look different than anyone else's because your hopes, your dreams, the way you see the world, the things that make your heart sing, and your most deeply held values are unique to you. This is why self-awareness is the cornerstone of Conscious Simplicity. We need awareness to notice when our words, actions or behaviors are not in alignment with who we are at our core. We also need the willingness to realign our inner and outer worlds when we notice they are not in harmony with each other. In order to stay true to our self we need to recognize and release the unnecessary distractions, the outside influences, and the inner and outer clutter that keep us from hearing our inner voice. Once we are able to hear that voice, we need to make it our intention to honor it. That is how we live authentically.

We have written this book with the intention of creating a deeper awareness of the many ways we unnecessarily clutter up our life, as well as how we can begin to consciously simplify it. Part of that awareness comes from understanding just how much we are energetically affected by the things with which we surround our self. In other words, how we are affected by what we choose to own, what activities, habits and relationships we choose to participate in, the stories we choose to tell our self, and really, anything we choose to allow into or keep in our life.

This book brings together practical, spiritual and energetic information as well as insights and tools to help you find awareness, intention, and understanding about your own inner and outer clutter. It is our sincere intention that you, the reader, will feel inspired by the stories and supported with the tools to make conscious choices and deliberate decisions about what you want in your life, as well as how to release what you don't. We hope this book will help empower you to move your life forward in whatever direction your heart desires.

Our Inspiration for Writing This Book

Barbara's Story -

After moving back home to Michigan from Indianapolis, Teresa established a women's group that met monthly. The women ranged in age from 22 to 70 and gathered together to gain knowledge, explore insights and share wisdom about various topics. When one of the members requested "clutter" as a meeting topic, Teresa invited me to join her in presenting to the group. As a professional organizer coach, I have a lot to say about clutter and how it affects us! Little did we know how our discussion of clutter would expand on that cold, wintry night in the comfort of Teresa's welcoming home. What began as a presentation about physical clutter, organizing, and simplifying, soon became a spirited discussion about much, much more. The floodgates opened as the women realized what they had been holding onto without considering why they were holding onto it, or how it affected them and held them back.

As we talked about how the energy of our physical possessions can affect us, many of the women began to make connections between our "outer clutter" and our "inner clutter." It became clear that symbols of broken relationships, of life chapters long since passed, of imagined significance, were occupying our spaces and keeping us stuck in unexpected ways. It also became clear that there was much more to the story.

Upon awakening in Teresa's guest room the next morning, I reflected on the previous evening. I could still feel the energy of the women who experienced a shift resulting from awareness and 'aha' moments. As I lay there my thoughts traveled to my home and I wondered, "What might I be mindlessly holding onto that no longer serves me, and is there any inner clutter connected to it?" As I did a mind's eye tour of each room in my home, I thought about the things I had on display and tucked away in various cabinets, cupboards, and closets. With a start I sat up and said, "The Jello molds!"

Quite excitedly, I got up and found Teresa in the kitchen making coffee. For the next several hours we consumed immeasurable amounts of caffeine and talked non-stop. We both felt the energy from the night before swirling around us, remembering all that took place and all the realizations the women had made. As we continued to engage in conversation about the meaning of our physical possessions, I told Teresa the story of the Jello molds.

Several years earlier while living in Florida, my late husband Gerry – who owned the kitchen and every activity associated with providing food for family and friends – wanted a Jello mold for a recipe he found. His unsuccessful search led him to talking with friends about his mission to locate a Jello mold somewhere. And as we know too well, the universe will answer our call when we are clear and intentional. The same week he stumbled upon a Jello mold and bought it, our neighbor delivered another one she found at a secondhand shop. We were all set with Jello molds. What I'm not sure about is if Gerry actually ever made that tempting recipe that launched his Jello-mold-seeking journey!

Within the year after Gerry died, I moved back to Indianapolis. The Jello molds came with me. I didn't want to take up precious kitchen space to store them so I placed them in the lovely built-in cabinets in my living room. Many times, I would go into the living room cabinet, mindlessly move the Jello molds to get what I needed and just as mindlessly put them back.

The curious thing is, I am a woman of multiple decades and I have never used a Jello mold or had any intention of creating any culinary delight with one. But I kept those molds, never really giving thought about them, other than where am I going to store them. What I realized that morning at Teresa's was I kept them because they were important to my husband. Yet they served no purpose in my life; I was hanging onto remnants of a previous life. I neglected to be mindful, to be conscious, about what I was keeping and why. It was freeing – freeing of space, freeing of "should,"– to return home, take a picture of the molds for memory sake and perhaps a humorous reminder of the situation, and donate them. I knew I had many other, more significant remembrances of my husband and the life we shared.

It was during that caffeine fueled morning, while revealing the numerous things we had been holding onto and talking about the stories of the remarkable women who were there the night before that we realized there was a bigger story to be told. We knew that most times it is not about the physical stuff. It's about our attachment to it and our relationship to it. And if we can better understand that attachment and relationship, we can make conscious choices about what is important to keep in our life. We were inspired that day to write this book.

TERESA'S STORY -

Barbara and I almost named this book "It's Not About the Jello Molds" because what became very clear as we talked that morning after the women's group gathering is that we can learn a lot about who we are by taking a deeper look at what we surround our self with, and we can gain a lot of insight into our inner world by becoming more aware of our outer world. What we found in the weeks following our gathering was that so many of us were continuing to have revealing insights about the things we'd been hanging onto and why. We discovered that we were energetically affected more than we had known by these things we had failed to let go, and we discovered that awareness of these physical things could lead us to some valuable information about what it was we were really hanging onto.

My own "aha" moment came toward the end of the gathering, as the women sat, sharing their stories, and it took me by complete surprise. I realized that, although it wasn't the only thing I had been hanging onto, there was one thing in particular I had not been able to release, even through six moves! This particular something that I had not been able to part with sat, packed in a box, on a shelf in my basement, gathering dust, out of sight and seemingly out of mind. And, although I hadn't used it in nearly a decade, I chose to pack it and haul it with me through each and every move.

That something was a hand painted water pitcher with four matching glasses that were given to me as a Mother's Day gift years before by my now grown sons. I did love that pitcher and those glasses very much at one time, and I displayed them in my kitchen for years, appreciating their beauty almost every day. Although I loved that they came from my sons who had given me such a thoughtful gift, I didn't really love the glassware so much anymore, and the pieces were obviously serving no purpose packed away in my basement. I wasn't loving them and I wasn't using them. So, why had I not been able to let them go, as much as I had tried, even after a half dozen moves? What was going on with me?

Sharing my thoughts with the women, I found myself becoming emotional, just as I had each of the times I had considered giving the pitcher and glasses away before. I recognized the guilt that always crept in when I thought about letting them go. But I also realized that I wanted that pitcher and those glasses to be enjoyed by somebody rather than boxed up in the basement, bringing pleasure to no one at all. Eventually, I retrieved the box from the basement, unwrapped the glassware and asked if any of the women would like them. As it turned out, one of the women, Marcy, fell in love with the set and said she had the perfect spot in her kitchen to display them. I told her they were hers and wrapped and boxed them back up for her. And then I cried.

Obviously this was not about the glassware! There had been many other Mother's Day gifts through the years, and I certainly had not saved them all. I was going to have to dig a little deeper to uncover what was coming up for me. What I had forgotten, but discovered again as I talked with Barbara the next morning, was that this particular Mother's Day gift was given to me shortly before I made the decision to leave my first marriage. The boys and their Dad had driven 45 minutes to a nearby town to buy them for me after I had admired them in a shop a few weeks prior. What they represented to me was a simpler and more innocent time in my sons' lives. A time when they were able to assume that their parents would always be together and that their family would always be intact. I had carried a lot of guilt over the years about complicating their lives with a divorce, a lot of which I had worked through and let go. But apparently there was more to be dealt with. The glassware was bringing up this old guilt I didn't even know I still carried, but that had been triggered each time I had tried to let that Mother's Day gift go. Fortunately, just coming to that awareness, and talking it through for a bit with Barbara, helped me to change my perspective. When I was able to hold my old wounds up to the light, I was able to see them differently and allow them to fully heal. What a gift I had received by looking a little deeper!

These are just two of our own personal stories from that wonderful, insightful evening that sparked this journey. We will be sharing more from clients and others we have worked with throughout this book, as well as more of our own, although we have changed the names out of respect for the privacy of those involved. We hope these stories will inspire you to embrace Conscious Simplicity, in whatever ways feel best to you, by becoming more aware of both the inner and outer clutter in your life and to begin to make more conscious choices about what you choose to hang onto.

CHAPTER 1

UNDERSTANDING CONSCIOUS SIMPLICITY

"Living consciously entails paying attention to the relationship between our professed values, goals, and purposes and our daily behavior."

~ NATHANIEL BRANDEN

WHAT IS CONSCIOUS SIMPLICITY

CONSCIOUS SIMPLICITY IS a way of living and a way of being in the world that is intentional and that creates the physical, emotional and energetic space that supports the life we want to live. Conscious Simplicity is the deliberate decision to stay fully aware of what we choose to allow into our life. It is also about the thoughtful letting go of what no longer serves us in order to make room for what our heart desires and a life that nourishes our soul. Conscious Simplicity is by no means about getting rid of everything we own or following anyone else's guidelines or expectations for life. It's also not about going without or depriving our self of the things we need and love. On the contrary, it's about enhancing our life by making conscious choices about what we want in it, and it's about making sure our stuff does not own us!

WHAT CONSCIOUS SIMPLICITY REQUIRES

"When you trust yourself, you will know how to live."

~ *GOETHE*

Conscious Simplicity requires that we trust life, and that we trust in our own ability to define what we really want in our life. It requires knowing that we are meant to be happy. We need to understand that the Universe has our back. It is here to support us in our deepest desires, but it needs to know what those desires are before it can fulfill them. It needs to know what we love, what we value, and what makes our heart sing. When we mindlessly accept and hang onto the things that are not in alignment with who we really are, life will continue to send us more of the same old stuff – the same old things, relationships, jobs, and financial and other issues we have gotten used to because that is the message and direction we have given it. When we step into Conscious Simplicity by making mindful choices about what we are willing to allow or keep in our life, we are giving life clear direction about our desires. That clear direction is what life needs in order to start sending us what we truly want.

WHEN LESS IS MORE, WHEN MORE IS LESS

When we make the conscious choice to simplify, to strip away the unnecessary and that which no longer represents or supports the life we wish to live, we tend to notice and appreciate what we do have more. When we make the conscious choice to have only what we love, what we use, and what brings beauty into our life; when we are not bogged down with that which has outlived its purpose in

2

our life, we make room to welcome in new and wonderful experiences that embody the life we are living now or the life we want to create for our self.

When we embrace Conscious Simplicity, we avoid the burden that comes with having too much stuff and focus much more on creating quality relationships, experiences, and expressions of who we really are, all of which then have the space to grow and expand in wonderful ways. We may have less stuff in our life, as well as less stuff going on in our life, but what we do have has been intentionally chosen. Our life feels richer, freer, more blessed, more beautiful, and more meaningful. Our soul feels so much more satisfied and we have opened the door to living our most authentic life.

Because we live in a profit driven world that bombards us with the constant message that "more is better," the very thought of having less of anything can trigger deeply held fears of scarcity, as well as fears of our own personal inadequacy. These fears can make the releasing process uncomfortable unless we stay conscious of what it is we are actually gaining in the process.

With that in mind, we invite you to entertain a seemingly small, but potentially powerful shift in perspective when you find the "more is better" mindset creeping in. We aren't suggesting that you necessarily and immediately attempt to undue the years of socialization that created the belief that more is better. If releasing that mindset doesn't seem to work for you right now, we suggest instead that you fully embrace it, only with a twist.

The truth is, more can be better! However, it isn't more "stuff" that is better, it's more space, more freedom, more time and more peace of mind that is better! All of which translates into the ability to focus on what we really want to create in our life. Know that with every unwanted, unloved, nonworking or simply outgrown item, relationship, activity or thought you release from your life, you are creating more freedom. Talk about immediate abundance!

It cannot be stated too many times that moving toward Conscious Simplicity isn't about getting rid of all of our earthly possessions or following someone else's rules of how we should live or what we should have. It's about making intentional choices that are right for us in this chapter of life, rather than blindly going along with how we've always lived in the past or how we think we are expected to live.

CHAPTER 2

AWARENESS

"Mindfulness is about being fully awake in our lives. It is about perceiving the exquisite vividness of each moment. We also gain immediate access to our own powerful, inner resources for insight, transformation, and healing."

~ JON KABAT-ZINN

EMBRACING CONSCIOUS SIMPLICITY requires taking our life off of autopilot and moving it into awareness. Not only an awareness of what we want for our self, but also an awareness of all the stuff that complicates our life, gets in our way, and keeps us stuck. As our life changes and evolves, the stuff that fills our life changes too. We just need to make room to allow the new to flow in easily and not become part of a burdened pile of stuff that serves to hold us back. When we move toward Conscious Simplicity we become more aware of what we allow into our life and why we keep it, whether it's physical possessions, relationships, habits, activities, thoughts or beliefs. When we become more aware, our perceptions begin to shift. Shifts in our perceptions create shifts in our thoughts and behavior, and transitions in both our inner and outer worlds. We begin to shift our life into Conscious Simplicity as we become more aware of the choices we are making in life.

Through awareness we can recognize what keeps us stuck and take conscious steps to break free of it, creating room in our life for the things, activities, experiences and relationships that support the life we want to live.

Linea's story (below) is an example of how embracing Conscious Simplicity requires us to get honest with our self about the things we are holding on to and what purpose, if any, they are really providing. If we are unable to honestly identify a purpose for something we are holding onto, even if that purpose is simply that it brings beauty or enjoyment into our life, we need to ask our self why we have not let it go.

Linea was a self-described "hopeless romantic" with a string of unsatisfying relationships under her belt. Long ago divorced with a demanding job and three daughters to raise on her own, she never gave up hope of finding a "true partner" to share her life. She dated and often things looked promising in the beginning, only to quickly go sour, leaving her baffled as to what was getting in her way of the happy, healthy, long term relationship she so desired.

When the topic of releasing the remnants of old relationships came up at the women's group meeting mentioned previously in the introduction, Linea remarked almost in passing that her garage was filled with boxes of mementos from every single relationship she had ever been in. Of course we couldn't help asking what was behind her inclination to allow the stuff of past relationships to take up valuable space in her present life. She answered that she didn't think it was a big deal since it was just out in the garage. She did admit however, that her garage was so full of boxes and other forgotten items that she had never actually been able to park in it.

As the evening went on Linea made some valuable connections between the physical items and the emotional stuff she had been holding onto from past relationships, and she became determined to let that old relationship clutter go and to reclaim her garage, as well as her heart space. She set a date for clearing, cleaning, and recycling, enlisted the help of her daughters, and got ready to clean out the garage with the conscious intention of "releasing the energy of past relationships." The next time we spoke with Linea, she was bubbling over with excitement. Not only was she able to park in her garage for the first time since she had moved in 10 years earlier, she had discovered enough sellable items that she decided to hold a garage sale and made enough money to buy the furniture she had been wanting for months. Not only had she saved herself valuable time and energy because parking in the garage meant no longer having to clear snow from her car each winter morning before work, she was loving her new furniture and looked forward to entertaining guests in her home for the first time in years. Linea felt like she had hit the jackpot!

Not surprisingly, shortly after she set out to consciously release the energy of those past relationships, someone new came into Linea's life. The last time we spoke, she was enjoying the new relationship, having fun and "keeping my heart open" to all the possibilities.

Awareness of what she was keeping in her life and how it impacted her both spatially and emotionally allowed Linea to release stuff from her past, make room for the new, and move toward Conscious Simplicity.

Becoming Aware of our Clutter

Becoming aware of both the physical and non-physical clutter that we allow to take up our valuable time, energy, and space is how we begin to empower our self to transform our life. In the following pages, we'll define physical clutter – the excess, the unnecessary, the things we keep in our life that are no longer useful to us, as well as non-physical clutter – the intangible and often less obvious ways we manage to clutter up our life.

According to the Online Etymology Dictionary, clutter is a variant of a 16th century word, clotern, which means, "to form clots, to heap on." How interesting that clutter is associated with clotting. When something clots it accumulates, it coagulates, it gets stuck, and is unable to move forward or flow freely. The various forms of clutter around us can have this same effect on our life. Whether physical or non-physical, anything that lowers our energy and keeps our environments, our psyches, and our life in that stuck position, unable to move forward, can be considered clutter.

We typically think of clutter just in terms of messes or too much stuff lying around, which can make it easy to overlook some of the less tangible clutter in our life. Not surprisingly, not everyone is affected by the various types of clutter in the same way. One person may feel energized by the very same item, activity or individual that another finds draining. Something that feeds one person's soul may feel like a burden on another. This is why self-awareness is so important and so empowering in this process. If we aren't aware of the clutter in our life, we certainly will not be aware of how it's affecting us. Let's take a look at some of the forms clutter can take.

Physical Clutter

Physical clutter includes the stuff we can see in our homes, our work places, our cars, and even our briefcases and purses. It's also the stuff that is packed away but still in our space, or even stuff that we pay to keep stored elsewhere. Physical clutter occurs for many reasons, and it remains for many reasons. Some are situational, such as life events that take us off track of our routines and makes it challenging to maintain organization. Sometimes clutter is due to more ongoing conditions, such as chronic disorganization, over-acquiring, overly busy schedules or simple overwhelm. We can get so overwhelmed with the scope of our stuff that we don't know where to begin de-cluttering it. Or we may no longer even notice that it's there, which makes it convenient to avoid. Clutter blindness is an actual phenomenon that causes a person's failure to see the clutter in front of them. They are exposed to the clutter long enough that they become numb to it and make no effort to remove it. An inability to see what's in front of us or know the first step to take can easily hold us back and keep us stuck.

Regardless of why physical clutter manifests, it can take many different forms, including:

- **Things we don't love or use**, but hang onto for a variety of reasons.
- **Things that are broken**, but that we've convinced our self we will fix someday.
- **Things that are unfinished**, but we keep because we're certain we will get to it one day.
- **Things that are left out**, either because they don't have a "home" or because there are no systems in place for putting them where they belong.
- **Things we keep "just in case."** Just in case we need it, someone else needs it, or we make an appearance on Let's Make A Deal.
- **Things needing a decision**. These are the things that accumulate when we delay deciding what to do with them. We haven't decided if we should fix it, toss it, donate it, put it away, or keep it just in case, so we do nothing.
- **Too much stuff in too small of a space**. This is actually a math problem.

- **Other people's stuff.** This is stuff belonging to the person(s) with whom we share our space.
- **Inherited clutter.** These are the things that have been passed onto us and that often carry a sizeable guilt factor when we think about letting them go.

NON-PHYSICAL CLUTTER

Non-physical clutter can be a little harder to identify particularly since we can't see it. It exists on a less tangible level and requires other senses to detect; yet it can be at least equally as disruptive to our life. Often we can feel that something is affecting our energy, sometimes by over-stimulating us, or sometimes by draining us, but we just keep plugging away without taking the time to consciously become aware of what it is we're feeling and why. We'll take a more in depth look at non-physical clutter and how to identify it in Chapter Eight. For now, let's simply take a look at some of the forms it can take.

Emotional and mental clutter impairs our ability to be happy and productive, and to focus on what's important to us. This can include the negative stories we tell our self and that we continue to tell our self until they become true for us; outdated beliefs we haven't examined or allowed to evolve; grudges, resentments and regrets resulting from the inability to forgive our self or others; guilt we refuse to release; an obsession with how we are perceived by others; relationships that drain our energy, and anything else that unnecessarily leaves us emotionally exhausted.

Communication clutter can lower our energy or leave us feeling over stimulated. It can include word clutter, resulting from talking too much or using more words than necessary in an attempt to impress or be noticed, or just out of nervousness; noise clutter such as keeping a TV or radio on to fill the silent spaces, rather than allowing our self to experience being alone with our thoughts; gossip clutter, which steals our time, zaps our energy and eventually makes us feel bad about our self either by listening to it, sharing it or both; e-clutter, which is evident in our in-boxes, phones, computers and various forms of social media; and information clutter which causes information overload with the availability of 24/7 news, commercials, pop up ads and other endless resources.

Additional types of non-physical clutter may include time clutter, resulting from failing to set boundaries for our time and energy; body clutter, which can be described as the things we mindlessly eat, drink or otherwise put into our bodies; financial clutter that shows up in the form of unpaid bills, unnecessary debt and/or a failure to act with financial integrity; and spiritual clutter that occurs when we go through the motions or blindly follow religious beliefs and practices, rather than examining them to ensure they resonate with us on a deeply spiritual level.

One form of non-physical clutter that eventually came blaring into Barbara's consciousness was communication clutter, specifically the noise clutter from TV and 24/7 news.

For many years part of my morning routine as I got ready for work was to turn on the TV and listen to the local news followed by the one of the national morning news programs. It was as predictable as making a pot of coffee and taking a shower, requiring no conscious thought to make it happen. Then I started to notice something. Many times I would start my work day feeling uneasy and hyper, and I wasn't sure why. I made an effort to pay attention to my thoughts and my body to discern what was going on. What I realized over time was that the endless chatter, the disturbing news stories, the tales of conflict definitely affected my mood. Even the "feel good" stories had an effect as I would stop and watch them, often at the expense of being on time.

I recognized also that many times the TV was on just to be on and that the noise for the sake of noise was not helpful. The only exception for me is during football and pro golf seasons – I love the sound of both sports coming from the TV even if I'm not watching them. I think they take me back to Sunday afternoons during my childhood with the family when we watched our favorite team and golfers play. So I tried an experiment and kept the TV off in the mornings and the results were delightfully surprising. Initially, I was convinced that without the morning weather report – 10 times over during the hour that I watched – and the national news, I would be rendered to being inappropriately dressed for the weather and ignorant of anything going on in the world. But I was wrong. A quick check of the weather on my smart phone told me all I needed to know. And it was impossible for anything of real importance to go unnoticed between news feeds and internet home pages.

What difference did turning off the morning TV make? I moved through my morning routine much more calmly. I listened to music or called a loved one during my walk with my dog. My days started more peacefully, more centered, and creative thoughts would surface. I was also able to prepare myself mentally as I consciously thought about what I wanted to accomplish and how I wanted to show up for my clients and for life. And I was on time!

What we've covered here is certainly no means all-inclusive, but it does paint a broader picture of some of the ways we may be unknowingly complicating our life with both physical and non-physical clutter. If you are starting to wonder about the connection between the physical and non-physical clutter in your life, much awareness about your inner world can be gained by taking a look at your outer world.

What Our Outer World Can Tell Us About Our Inner World

Have you ever walked into a cluttered room and noticed how you feel? It's probably a safe bet a cluttered room does not feel uplifting, relaxing, or invigorating because the energy of the room affects our energy. Our outer world and inner world reflect each other and when one is disorderly, the other is often disorderly too. Where physical clutter exists, emotional and mental clutter are not far behind and vice versa. Clear one and the other will typically follow. At the very least, it will clear more easily and readily. Teresa was able to witness an amazing example of this with a family she worked with several years ago.

I met Bonnie when I was a Social Worker and was assigned her case. At the time, she was living in a women's shelter and her three young children had been temporarily placed in foster care due to extreme domestic violence in the home. As her husband awaited trial on spousal and child abuse charges, Bonnie filed for divorce and began taking steps to rebuild her life and reunite with her children. She was a gentle soul, who clearly loved and missed her children, and although she struggled with depression and posttraumatic stress from the years of abuse, she was determined to do whatever it took to keep her children together.

When her ex-husband was convicted and sent to prison, Bonnie was finally able to return to the family home and begin the process of reuniting with her children. While the court determined that the children could be safely returned to Bonnie's custody, they also decided to keep support services in place while the family pieced their lives back together. Because of this, I met regularly with Bonnie and her children in the family home during the next eighteen months.

During the course of that time, I was able to witness Bonnie gain confidence and a belief in herself that she had never had before. A former stay-at-home Mom, she found work at a local specialty bakery, received training, and eventually worked her way up from cashier to head baker, saving every penny she could along the way. With each accomplishment her confidence grew. While parenting three children alone, maintaining a home and working long, non-traditional hours at the bakery was sometimes overwhelming for Bonnie, she was very grateful for the life she was building for herself and her family. Through it all, she managed to also find the time to continue with both individual and family counseling as she and her children worked to heal from the emotional and physical abuse they had endured at the hands of her ex-husband.

While there were ups and downs in her healing process, I was able to quite accurately assess Bonnie's state of mind each week, as soon as I saw the condition of her home. When Bonnie was feeling positive, strong and hopeful, the house would reflect that. When she was feeling overwhelmed, sad, or struggling in other ways, the state of the house would also reflect that. During my earlier home visits, Bonnie's house was often extremely cluttered and chaotic. At times it was even difficult to find a place to sit with all the clothes, dirty dishes and even bags of garbage strewn about in every room. Often, blinds would be drawn, lights would be burned out and there was an overall gloomy feeling that was hard to miss.

As the weeks and months went by and Bonnie's family began to heal and transform their lives, I couldn't help but notice their home transforming too. During one of my final visits, I was pleased to find blinds open, lights on and a noticeable absence of clutter. Bonnie laughed as she proudly told me the story of how she and the children had spent the past two weekends de-cluttering, cleaning and organizing, and how she had rewarded them all with a special pizza and movie night at home. There was a palpable change in the energy of their home from that day forward and I believed I had witnessed a turning point for the family.

Several weeks later, on my last visit to Bonnie's home, that belief was strengthened when she greeted me at the door with a smile and paint roller in her hand. "I just finished painting the kitchen and living room," she said excitedly. "Goodbye to that dingy old grey!" She grinned and waved her hand toward the freshly painted, yellow walls. As I acknowledged how busy she had been, I asked what got into her. She answered, "I don't know. I just wanted a change and felt like it was time for some color in my life." We laughed some more and joked about the brightness of the yellow paint she had chosen, but I took it all as a very good sign that Bonnie had turned another corner in her healing process. Bonnie and her home had gone from dark, dingy, chaotic and cluttered, to bright, cheery, relatively clutter free and much more peaceful. Something had obviously shifted in her life, and although many things factored into this turning point, Bonnie was clearly in good place that day. Both her inner and outer environments reflected that. I left feeling confident that she and her family were going to find their way.

While Bonnie's case is extreme, it is a good example of just how much our outer world reflects what's going on in our inner world. Taking an honest look at the state of our environment can, no doubt, bring valuable insight into the state of our psyches. What comes to mind when you look around your own home? If this were the home of someone you had never met and knew nothing about, what might it tell you about them and their state of mind, and what they value most in life?

CHAPTER 3

CLUTTER ENERGY

"Whether it's people, places or things, be selective in when, where and how you invest your precious time, money and energy."

~ELEANOR BROWNN

CLUTTER ENERGY AND HOW IT CAN AFFECT US

VERY OFTEN WE are not consciously aware of how we are physically, emotionally and energetically affected by the clutter in our life, but it can affect us in multiple ways. When we surround our self with possessions, relationships, activities, thoughts and beliefs that do not bring value to our life, we create clutter energy. The result is we often find our self stuck and unable to move our life forward, as clutter energy typically ties us to the past and prevents us from creating the present and future we desire. Clutter energy is the physical, emotional, and mental drain we experience when we surround our self with things that do not serve our highest purpose.

Because we've been conditioned to see life from only a physical perspective, we can easily forget that *everything* in our world is just energy in varying form. But when we are able to also see the world from an energetic perspective and remember that everything is, in fact, energy, we can begin to see our world, our stuff, and our self differently. We can begin to see how our thoughts, emotions, spirits, bodies, and our life are connected to and can be affected by the energetic frequency of everything around us.

Many individuals burdened with their stuff say they are "sick and tired" of the mess and are overwhelmed, stressed, and confused about where to begin to sort through the clutter. Research supports the validity of those comments. Following a nine-year project conducted by a UCLA study with 32 California families, a link was discovered between depression and the amount of stuff in our homes. Princeton University Neuroscience Institute conducted research that showed the presence of clutter can cause the brain to feel overwhelmed and unable to focus. Furthermore, constantly trying to find things in a cluttered state steals valuable time, resulting in frustration and irritation, sometimes even risking a drain on our finances from a vicious cycle of buying, losing, buying, losing. For these reasons and more, clutter energy can actually cause fatigue, make us feel sick, and result in lowered self-esteem and confidence.

Clutter energy can also cause disharmony in relationships. It can happen when one member of a household demonstrates clutter behavior and another does not, or it can happen when multiple individuals in a home lead cluttered lifestyles. In addition, clutter energy can cause isolation and limit the opportunities for friendships when we are embarrassed to invite anyone over.

Clutter energy distracts us from focusing on the things that are important to us in life. Whether we are aware of it or not, we are profoundly affected by our surroundings and when our surroundings are filled with clutter, whether physical or non-physical, our minds feel cluttered too. Even if we are seemingly successful at tuning out the clutter of our life, it takes valuable energy to do so, energy that could be put to better use on the things we genuinely value. Clutter energy can keep us from new relationships, new jobs, new experiences. Basically, it can prevent us from moving forward in life. And as it blocks anything new from coming into our life, it blocks us from giving all of our self to life.

Because all environments are charged with their own unique energy, we absorb and experience the energy of the places we spend time in. When our environments contain clutter, we absorb and experience the clutter energy in both subtle and not so subtle ways. If you doubt that you are picking up the energy of the places you spend time in, just think about how differently you feel walking into a church as opposed to a basketball stadium; a library as opposed to a cocktail lounge; or a hospital as opposed to a movie theatre. The energy of each space is clearly different and you feel different in each space, whether you register it consciously or not. To heighten your awareness about the effect of clutter energy, we invite you to notice the difference in how you feel simply walking from a cluttered space into to an uncluttered space in your own home, or vice versa. Becoming aware of the clutter energy in your life and how it affects you is key to embracing Conscious Simplicity.

Teresa got a clear reminder of how clutter energy can affect us when she and her husband, Dave, contracted to have their old deck torn down and a new one built. Thankfully, the clutter in this case was temporary and so were the effects on her, but it surely brought in to her awareness just how much energy it takes to tune out the clutter in our life.

Expecting that some chaos would come along with the construction, I prepared myself in advance and felt grateful that it would be happening outside where I thought I could ignore it for the two weeks the contractor estimated it would take. However, those two weeks turned into two months of lumber piles, wood scraps, trash, power tools and other equipment randomly strewn about our back and side yards. It was almost impossible to walk through our garage where more lumber and power tools were placed, let alone park a car in it, and the noise and intrusions on my time seemed to never stop. It would be fair to say there was lots of clutter energy going on at my house during this time.

Because our contractor had underestimated the time frame and seemed incapable of ever arriving on schedule, he ended up staying until dark most evenings, which meant the noise and chaos continued well past dinnertime. Since I work from home and Dave works out of town during the week, overseeing this project was mostly my responsibility and, trust me, it wasn't going well! Although I did my best to roll with it all, I vented my frustrations more than once to both Dave and the contractor, who promised on a daily basis to do better, but never did. In the end, we had to let him go and find someone else to finish the job.

When it was finally over and my home was once again a quiet, mostly clutter-free and peaceful place to be, I realized just how much I had been affected by living with that chaos for over two months. Of course I was frustrated with the contractor for various reasons, but it was more than that. I realized that what I came to call my "two-month home invasion" had really knocked me off center. My sanctuary, my retreat when the world is too crazy-busy-noisy for me, the place I count on to help ground me, nurture my soul and remind me of who I really am, had been temporarily invaded, and I was surely feeling the effects of it. It would be accurate to say that I was over stimulated and stressed out by the clutter, noise and chaos that had been surrounding me for so many weeks. Sleepless nights, a lack of ability to focus, and a visible reduction in my energy level was just some of what I experienced over the course of those weeks. I also found that as my stress level increased, my productivity level decreased and I had difficulty completing much beyond the most routine tasks. And, according to Dave, I was apparently a little grumpy at times. Go figure!

What was most interesting to me though was that while I was aware of some frustration and stress throughout the process, I honestly had no idea *how strongly I had been affected until it was over and peace was once again restored to my home. It seems the noise, chaos, and clutter had started to feel normal to me after I'd been in the midst of it for a while, although it certainly never felt good. It absolutely makes me wonder how often we fail to fully notice how strongly we're affected by our surroundings and how often we just grow used to the clutter energy in our life.*

While the chaos and clutter energy I experienced during the deck construction most likely did not cause me or anyone else any long-term effects, in cases of extreme clutter, the consequences can be very high. Having spent many years working in the field of child welfare, I have witnessed some of the most extreme cases of clutter, as well as some of the most devastating effects it can have on families. Watching a family lose their home, or a child placed in foster care because the home simply becomes so cluttered that it is deemed unsafe to inhabit, is heartbreaking. Even with assistance and counseling, some of the parents I worked with were either unwilling or unable to let go of the clutter that threatened their own safety and that of their children. Sadly, I saw families permanently ripped apart because of it more than once. Of course those cases were the most extreme of the extreme and those involved had deeper issues going on, such as severe depression, unprocessed grief, addictions or mental illness, but they are forever etched in my mind and left me wondering how we ever came to believe that we could fill our inner emptiness with more things, more substances or more distractions.

What we do know is that our souls hunger for an authentic, meaningful and conscious life and, try as we might to fill that hunger from outside of our self, it simply can't be done. Eventually the excess in our life just becomes a burden on our energy, taking us even further away from who we really are. But when we slow down, simplify, pay attention and clear the space in our life to consciously align with the deeper desires of our heart, life becomes richer, more authentic and much more satisfying. When we take the time to sincerely ask what it is we are really hungering for, rather than mindlessly trying to fill that hunger with more, more, more, we open the door for true nourishment and fulfillment of our soul. This requires a willingness to clear the stuck energy from our life. We will talk more about how to do that in Chapters Six and Eight, but for now let's take a look at what might be keeping that clutter energy stuck.

WHAT KEEPS THE CLUTTER ENERGY STUCK

"Fear and pain should be treated as signals not to close our eyes, but to open them wider."

~ NATHANIEL BRANDEN

Becoming aware of what's keeping the clutter energy stuck requires some self-examination. Whether we are conscious of it or not, there are usually deeper reasons why we hang on to the things we hang on to in life. We can chalk it all up to bad luck, fate, simply not having the time to do what we need to do, or any variety of other reasons outside of our control, but there are valuable insights to be gained by taking an honest look at what's preventing us from releasing what no longer serves us and moving into the life we want to live.

So, what is it that keeps the clutter energy stuck? It starts with the premise that we live either from a place of love or a place of fear. While love is our natural state of being, fear has been learned. Fear and love cannot occupy the same space. There is only room for one at a time. No matter what form it takes, fear is often at least a part of what keeps the clutter energy stuck.

Often, we are prompted to try to soothe the fear by bringing in or holding onto more stuff rather than taking a look at what our fear could show us. We fear the unknown and hold onto the past because it's known and there is a comfort in that, regardless if it's good or bad. We fear we won't have enough. We fear others will judge us for not having enough. We fear making a wrong decision. We fear feeling guilty about letting go of an item because of the money we spent on it or because someone dear gave it to us. We are afraid of being alone or vulnerable without our stuff. We are afraid that we are defined by our stuff and question, "Who would I be without these things?" So we hang onto the stuff, the thoughts, the beliefs, the relationships, the habits that once had a purpose in our life, but that no longer support who we are and the life we want to live now. And with all that stuff bogging us down, we risk staying stuck right where we are, rather than simplifying and moving forward.

A fear of intimacy can also be what's lurking behind the clutter energy. Our stuff can build a protective barrier that, if dismantled, may cause uneasiness. It is not unusual for individuals to say that once they clear out their clutter and create open space, they feel vulnerable. It's as if a shield has been removed and they are left feeling exposed and uncomfortable without it. Fortunately, while there may be an adjustment period, most experience the benefit of the uncluttered space, come to enjoy the freedom that accompanies it, and find it motivating to continue on.

Often we are not even aware of the fears that lie behind our resistance to letting go of our stuff, but the awareness that comes with examining our resistance can bring those fears into the light and help us move forward. Teresa discovered this at a particularly challenging time in her life.

Two years after my husband and I were married the company he worked for was sold, and we were transferred from Michigan, where I had grown up and raised my sons, to Columbus, Ohio. This happened just as our sons, who had all recently graduated from college, began building their own careers in different cities, one in Grand Rapids, Michigan, one in Chicago, and one on the west coast. As much as I wanted to see our sons follow their dreams and find their own way in the world, and as ready as I felt for a change in my own life, I was shaken by all the changes, and especially by the thought of us all living in different states. College was one thing, but this felt really permanent. This was not how I had envisioned our future and a part of me felt like the ground beneath my feet was crumbling. Still, I was determined to stay positive about what lay ahead and to put my energy into creating a beautiful new home for my husband and myself to enjoy and for our sons to visit when they could.

"I can do this!" I kept telling myself with a mixture of fear and excitement. And I held it together pretty darn good, through the house sale, the sorting and packing, the goodbyes, the closing on the new house, and the actual move. I was quite proud of how much I had been able to let go of in the process too. (There's nothing like the thought of packing and loading a U-Haul with everything you own to shine a little light on the excess in your life.) But what happened the day we unpacked the U-Haul in Columbus caught both my husband and me by surprise.

As we set up the dining room table and four matching chairs in our new and somewhat small dining room, I noticed a sinking feeling in the pit of my stomach. Four chairs were not enough for a family gathering! "Where are my extra chairs?" I asked my husband, frantically. "We'll need them when the boys come for Christmas!" "I put them up in the attic," he answered, innocently enough. "We can get them down when the boys come." And ... that's when I lost it. An honest to goodness, foot stomping, fist pounding, ear piercing, Tasmanian devil melt down is what I had. "NO!" I shrieked. "I need those chairs down and I need them down now!" My husband, who was looking at me like an evil alien had invaded his wife's body, tried to reason with me. "The holidays are six months away," he said. "I promise I'll get them down in plenty of time." But, I was not to be reasoned with and I was not taking no for an answer on this. I dug my heels in like a spoiled two-year-old who'd been denied a lollypop, and demanded my chairs. This was not one of my finer moments but one thing was certain, those extra chairs were coming down from the attic before sundown, even if I had to climb up there myself to get them. I needed my extra chairs! And so down they came. My husband retrieved the chairs and placed them in the garage, where they sat, unused, taking up valuable space and gathering dust, until we were unexpectedly transferred again, just 3 months later. This time to Indianapolis.

The day after my meltdown, alone in the new house and having rested up, I really had to take a look at what prompted my Tasmanian devil impersonation. Why was I so panic stricken about not having those extra chairs at my fingertips? There was nothing special about them. They were old, rather uncomfortable and not particularly pleasing to the eye. I knew the holidays were months away and there were actually no firm plans for the boys to come to Ohio yet anyway. There was also virtually no chance of the three of them arriving unexpectedly on my doorstep for a home cooked meal and catching me without enough chairs on hand. So, what was up with this panic? One thing was clear; this was not about the chairs!

That night, when my husband came home from work, we were able to talk things through on a much more rational level. As my tears began to spill out, so did a bucket full of fears. Fears about losing my connection with my sons, fears about never being able to prepare another Christmas Eve breakfast for the entire family again (one of our favorite traditions), and my deepest fear of all, that by moving away from our home town, I was somehow depriving my sons of a "home base," even though they had all moved first. Oh the stories we tell our self!

My epic meltdown had forced me to look deeper at what was going on inside of me. Along with the fears, I had a lot of guilt and sadness to process. I had been so busy preparing for the move and keeping a stiff upper lip that I hadn't taken the time to allow myself to feel what I was feeling. Those chairs represented something precious to me, not only my connection with my sons, but also their connections with each other. It was like I had convinced myself that our connections as a family were dependent upon keeping those old chairs! I couldn't help but wonder if we would ever all gather around that dining room table at the same time again, and that made me really sad. I was grieving for what I thought I had lost, or was in danger of losing, and this was important information for me to have. Some of my fears were valid, some were completely irrational, but all of them deserved to be held up to the light and allowed to heal, rather than stuffed down inside me, wreaking havoc on my peace of mind and scaring the hell out of my husband. Boy did I have some things to look at!

I tell you this story to demonstrate just how complicated our attachments to possessions can become when fear is involved, and just how much insight we can gain from taking a conscious look at our resistance to letting them go. I learned a lot about myself when I was willing to look at my attachment to those old chairs, and I did a lot of healing in the process. We have moved several times since that first move to Columbus and, somewhere along the way, I let go of those chairs. I don't even remember when or where. What I will not be forgetting though, is that what I value most in life, my connection with my family, was not dependent upon me having those chairs at my fingertips. And, by the way, somehow we all ended up living within a few, short hours of each other again, having missed only one Christmas Eve breakfast together. And, while that made me sad at the time, it certainly didn't change the connection we have as a family. What a testimony to love over fear!

Sometimes our fear shows up in another form and we find our self holding onto things because we are afraid we will lose our identity without them. Such was the case with Debra.

Though retired for several years, Debra admitted to holding onto a basement full of papers and supplies from her 30-year teaching career, including file cabinets and boxes full of ditto papers. (For those of you under 35 years old, you may need to do a Google search to learn what this is!). Debra had, at one point, started the process of clearing out those old dittos and other teaching supplies, but had stopped when it became uncomfortable for her. However, when challenged to look a little deeper at what was coming up for her, she realized that this was not about the dittos!

What Debra came to realize is that those outdated dittos and other teaching supplies represented a part of her identity that she had not been ready to let go. Having been a teacher for more than thirty years, she was not quite sure who she was outside of her profession. Somewhere in Debra's mind, the contents of those boxes and file cabinets represented "proof" of who she was and validated her life. Letting them go was uncomfortable, if not downright scary, because it required taking a look one of her biggest fears, the fear losing her identity.

When Debra took the time to understand why she had been holding onto these remnants of her teaching career, she was able to see some things from a new perspective. She realized what it was she was really afraid to let go of, her identity as a Teacher. With that awareness Debra began to move forward. She came to understand that getting rid of those papers would not negate her teaching career, her identity or her value as a human being. She had devoted more than three decades to the profession she loved and made a difference in the lives of countless students. Nothing was going to change that and she certainly didn't need to hold onto old paperwork to prove her life thus far had been of value. Still, Debra's "identity crisis" left her wondering what she wanted next in life and she knew she had some soul searching to do.

It has been fun to watch Debra's life expand since that time. She continues to discover and explore parts of herself she previously didn't even know existed, she loves to travel and she is having more new experiences and adventures than most people half her age. Oh, and, we might also add that, at the age of 72, Debra has fallen in love and is enjoying what she refers to as "the best relationship of my life." It appears her "identity" is doing just fine these days.

As Barbara also discovered with one of her clients, as well as with herself, even when we willingly release who we once were, we can find our self afraid to let go of those things that defined a previous chapter in our life.

Samantha wanted help de-cluttering and organizing her house before the arrival of their second child. The project involved converting the home office to her toddler's room to make room in the nursery for the baby. The office closet contained several women's suits that Samantha wore at her corporate job, something she thoroughly disliked and would never return to doing. She had since established a successful at-home career and suits were definitely not part of her daily wardrobe. Samantha was reluctant to get rid of the suits and when I asked what purpose the suits held for her current life, she couldn't answer. It took her several moments to realize the suits had once defined her professionally and even though she had no fond feelings or memories of her corporate experience, the suits represented an accomplished career. Being able to identify their meaning to her and realize they no longer represented who she was or what she wanted to do, made it much easier to donate all of them to a women's charity organization and allowed Samantha to experience conscious simplicity.

I certainly didn't judge her about holding onto to the suits as long as she did. It would have been inappropriate – not just from a professional perspective, but also from personal experience. I told Samantha about the wardrobe of business suits I kept after leaving my corporate career. But I didn't just keep them. I moved them with me when I relocated to Florida. I'm sure I was thinking there would be tremendous need for business suits in southwest Florida where I was planning to semi-retire. Yes. I was sure of that. So I stored them in a portable garment closet in our attic. I cannot recall one time I wore any of them. But I still didn't let them go. The suits came back with me when I returned to Indiana! It wasn't until I recognized I didn't have the luxury of storage space for them that I was forced to examine why I still had them. Until that point they "followed" me wherever I went, inappropriate as they were to the Florida life I was living and the professional organizing and coaching business I started when I moved back to Indiana. Those suits were a statement about who I was and what I accomplished in a previous time of my life and I was reluctant to let go of that. But the lack of space as well as the launch of my business demanded I let go of what was and make room for my new identity and my new adventure. That awareness allowed me to not only release those clothes, but to fully embrace my new journey and step into it completely. It was a very freeing exercise.

In addition to fear, a lack mentality is also often behind the stuck clutter energy. Just as love and fear cannot occupy the same space, the same is true for lack and abundance. If we believe we are in a state of lack, we are unable to see abundance in our life. When we walk in abundance consciousness, our heart feels full and a full heart will emanate love. A lack mentality leaves us empty and opens the space for fear to consume us. This comes from a lack of trust that we will have what we need when we need it. When we fear that our needs won't be provided for, we often hang on tight to everything we do have, whether it serves us or not. This is often the case if we have experienced great lack or poverty at an earlier time in our life and are bound and determined not to be caught lacking again. Sometimes we hang on to what we have, whether it be possessions, unhealthy relationships or unsatisfying jobs, because we just don't believe that anything better can come into our life.

When we don't feel that the Universe is here to support us, we operate from a lack mentality and cling to what we have. The irony is that our lack of trust and our inability to let go will pretty much guarantee that we will remain stuck, right where we're at, with nothing new coming into our life. This is the thinking that leads to the closets and storage areas full of things "just in case". Lack of trust breeds a negativity that easily becomes a self-fulfilling prophecy, further preventing us from living the best life we can. Conversely, an abundance perspective that trusts we will have what we need, when we need it, allows us to relax the firm grasp of everything around us and remain open to receiving what is important to us.

A lack of forgiveness is another way we keep the clutter energy stuck. We hold onto things that were a mistake to acquire in the first place and rather than forgiving our self and letting go, we keep it. Or we don't really like it but because we spent so much money on it, we keep it as we beat our self up every time we look at it. We think that maybe at some point we will find a need for it or actually use it, neither which are likely. And whether we keep it or donate it, the money has already been spent and will not be recovered. Better it be in someone else's possession who will use and value it than stuck away unwanted or unused in our space.

Maybe we withhold forgiveness because someone, somewhere in our past, a parent, a spouse, a sibling, once discarded our stuff without our permission. Our hurt and our anger for the total disregard for our feelings and our possessions cause us to dig in our heels and proclaim no one can make us get rid of anything again. We'll show them! Or, perhaps we hold a grudge towards another and let our clutter become an emotional crutch between us. On a subconscious level we think if the stuff is gone and no longer the point of contention, we may need to deal with the real issues we have with an individual or situation. And, we might have to take an honest look at some uncomfortable emotions in the process.

Sometimes we withhold forgiveness simply because we have been hurt. The night of our women's group gathering one woman discovered that a ring she'd been holding onto from a past romantic relationship was reflective of her lack of forgiveness for her former partner, and a clear indicator of some pretty serious clutter energy.

For more than two years, Linda held onto a ring given to her during a relationship that ended in heartbreak and betrayal. It wasn't a particularly valuable ring and it served no positive purpose in her current life, yet somehow she resisted letting it go. The breakup had been an especially difficult one and Linda admitted that each time she looked at the ring, she was reminded of how foolish she felt for trusting someone who clearly turned out to be untrustworthy. However, until we talked about how the ring made her feel, and why she might be keeping it, Linda had not even been consciously aware of the energy that ring held for her. Once she became aware of the connection between that ring and her state of mind, she felt more and more compelled to release it and the energy surrounding it from her life. This is not to say that it was easy for Linda. She struggled with mixed emotions. Part of her wanted to be free from the pain of her past, and part of her wanted to hang onto the pain as a reminder not to allow herself to be hurt again. It was as if hanging onto her anger and pain of the past would protect her from any future pain. An interesting trade off, even if life did actually work that way.

Within a few days of the women's group meeting, Linda enlisted the support of a good friend and together they made an event out of selling the ring to a second hand shop, then treated themselves to a fancy lunch with the proceeds. Linda greatly enjoyed that lunch for several reasons, not the least of which was that fine dining was something she had denied herself for quite some time. Actually, ever since her former partner had deemed such luxuries to be frivolous.

Linda described feeling lighter and more hopeful after becoming aware of the clutter energy surrounding that ring she'd been holding onto, and ultimately letting it go, and said it was an important step in her healing process. She had held onto it like she held onto her anger, pain and distrust, and making a conscious decision to release it felt quite empowering to her. It may have only been a small, physical object, but that ring was part of a bigger picture because of the stuck energy surrounding it and the meaning she had attached to it.

Obviously one ring does not take up much physical space, but when it ties us to a painful past, as it did with Linda, it tends to keep us stuck and takes up our valuable emotional space. By releasing the ring, Linda was making a statement to herself and to the Universe that she was ready to take her power back, move her life forward, and begin opening her heart to forgiveness, which we'll talk more about in Chapter Five.

As we heighten our awareness from a purely physical perspective to a physical *and* energetic perspective and become more aware of our own clutter energy, we are much better equipped to make conscious choices about what we are willing to have or keep in our life. When we are able to release what doesn't serve our highest good, we make room for that which does and that is when we begin to shift the energy of our life. Awareness, intention, understanding, and action will replace the fear that keeps the energy stuck and holds us back from fully living in the present. We'll be talking more about this in upcoming chapters, as well as the preparation and process of releasing both the physical and non-physical clutter in our life. Releasing our physical clutter will automatically bring about a shift in the energy of the space and a shift in our own personal energy as well, but we may even want to go one-step further and consider performing an intentional energy shifting ritual.

Shifting the Clutter Energy with a Ritual

An intentional energy shifting ritual is just what it sounds like, an intentional way to change the stagnant or stuck energy in an object, room or an entire house or building in order to get the positive energy flowing again. You could think of it as an energetic housecleaning for both yourself and your space, as well as a powerful statement that you are ready for a change.

Recently divorced and anxious to move her life forward, Julie had already done the work of releasing a lot of the physical clutter that was left behind when her marriage ended. Julie's former husband, James, had taken most of his personal possessions with him when he moved out of their shared home, and she had sold or given away much of those he chose to leave behind. But she did not stop there. When she was ready, Julie chose to let go of even the most intimate ties to their relationship. She sold her wedding ring, disposed of the birthday and anniversary cards James had given her throughout the years, as well as a box full of other mementos she had saved during the course of their relationship. This was done lovingly, not out of anger or resentment, and not to negate what was good about their marriage, but out of a sincere desire for a fresh start. Still, there was something about the energy of their formerly shared home that Julie had trouble shaking. James had been a sullen and controlling man, very critical of Julie and very vocal about his disapproval of almost all of her friends and family. Although their home was beautiful, there was still a palpable "heaviness" lurking somewhere within its energy that clearly did not feel very welcoming.

Having taken so many steps to move her life forward, and not one to accumulate or hang onto a lot of unnecessary possessions, Julie came to the women's gathering that evening, interested in supporting the other women, but not really feeling that the topic was particularly relevant to her. However, as the evening went on, and many of the women made connections about the clutter energy surrounding some of the things they had been hanging onto, Julie had her own "aha" moment about the clutter energy still lingering in her own home.

In the days that followed the gathering, Julie dug deeper into her heart's desires and gained more clarity about what she wanted for herself. She was in the process of rediscovering herself and she wanted her home to reflect who she was, what she loved, and what she valued most in life. She wanted her friends and family to feel welcomed, cherished and loved when they visited and she wanted to feel happy to be there even when she was alone. Her desire to make her home a welcoming place prompted her to invite friends over for an energy shifting celebration. Friends gathered in support of Julie as she stated her intention to "lovingly clear any energy that is not in alignment with my highest good and make this home a container for love, fun, peace and laughter." And then there was dancing, wine, and plenty of belly laughs.

While performing an energy shifting celebration may not seem like life changing events, it certainly felt empowering to Julie. She still identifies that conscious choice as one of the key steps in the process of reclaiming her sense of self and her power after her marriage ended. Her home and her life are now filled with the things that matter most to her and the energy there feels so welcoming that Julie often finds herself reveling in the role of host to friends and family,

What to keep and what to release when a relationship ends is a personal choice, but as Julie discovered it is a choice to be made consciously. The decision to intentionally shift the energy of your space is another personal choice to be made consciously and in Julie's case it was a choice that brought her peace of mind and helped her enjoy her home more.

Obviously, after you've cleared the physical clutter from your space is a good time to consider performing an energy shifting ritual or celebration, but almost any time you want to change the energy of an object or space is a good time. Let's take a look at some other times you might want to consider intentionally shifting the energy of your space.

- When you move into a new home or office building
- After a break up
- After a job loss
- After an illness or surgery
- When you've experienced a trauma
- After an argument
- When you are feeling stuck or in a funk
- When you simply cannot remove an unwanted object from your home or property
- Before or after weight loss.
- Anytime you simply want to make a change or move your life forward

There are plenty of books and plenty of resources on the Internet if you are interested in learning more about performing an energy shifting/energy clearing ritual in your own home. To help get you started we have provided information, Performing an Energy Shifting Ritual, in the Resources section. You don't need any special skills or training to perform an energy shifting, and although we have outlined some helpful steps, following them is not nearly as important as starting with a clear intention and trusting your own instincts. Don't let yourself get bogged down with the details or worry about doing it right, and don't be afraid to customize your ritual with some of your own tweaks. For instance, Teresa likes to play music and dance her way through the shifting. Have some fun with it. Actually, laughter is known to be the fastest way to shift the energy of anything, so don't be afraid to get goofy. You can certainly do this alone, but inviting a supportive friend or two (or even more) to join you can make it more fun and even more powerful. Remember, as long as you start with a clear intention to shift the energy of your space, or even of a particular object, and follow your instincts, you can't go wrong. Intention is everything as we will discover in the next chapter.

CHAPTER 4

INTENTION SETTING FOR CONSCIOUS SIMPLICITY

"When you're clear about your purpose and your priorities, you can painlessly discard whatever does not support these, whether it's clutter in your cabinets or commitments on your calendar."

~ VICTORIA MORAN

ASSESSING THE GAP BETWEEN READINESS AND WILLINGNESS

AT ONE TIME I (Barbara) thought the phrase 'ready and willing' seemed redundant, and used simply as a point of emphasis. Through my work with clients, I've become attuned to the distinction between ready and willing and the impact both have on a desired outcome. Many times individuals will call to say they are ready to get rid of the stuff, ready to clear their environments, ready to change their life. Yet there is an uncertainty, a resistance, a fear connected to their words that go beyond not knowing how to do it. Through conversation we discover that it is the gap between readiness and willingness. Unquestionably they are ready for the change, but there is uncertainty in their willingness to do the work necessary to accomplish that change.

Because decisions will be necessary and behavior changes will be essential, they can be reluctant to commit to doing the work that is required. What happens when readiness and willingness are not in alignment? Nothing. Fear will take over. The familiar and the same old, same old become the default mode.

Assessing the gap can be as basic as asking yourself, "On a scale of 1 to 10, how ready am I? And on that same scale, how willing am I to do what is necessary?" When there is a gap, spending time to understand why it is important to do the work and what we will gain or benefit from it can help reconcile the disconnect between the two. In other words, the gap closes with our intention. Sometimes we are able to do this on our own, and sometimes we need to enlist the help of another to get us where we want to go.

It's not uncommon to find a gap between our readiness and our willingness in any number of areas in our life, including consciously simplifying. While the benefits of embracing Conscious Simplicity may sound inviting, the truth is there is work involved, especially in the beginning. And, although the results may be immediately felt in some instances, in others the road ahead might appear a little daunting. Luckily, there are tools to help you get where you are going. Let's take a look at how setting a clear intention can help.

THE IMPORTANCE OF A CLEAR INTENTION

Whatever we are doing in life, from the most mundane daily chores to the great big, life-changing decisions, we need to be clear about the outcome we want. Setting our intention keeps us mindful of why we are doing what we are doing, and that alone brings a deeper meaning to anything we do. When we take the time to get clear about what we want and what it will bring us, we set an intention that will serve us well along the way. That's because when it comes to consciously simplifying our space and our life, knowing what we want and why we want it will not only remind us of what it is we are really trying to make happen, but it will help keep us on track. With that intention in place it's much easier to regroup and move forward when we feel stuck, get tired or discouraged, or otherwise lose our way.

Paying Attention to What You Desire

Setting a clear intention requires paying close attention to the callings of our heart. It can be easy to dismiss our desires as unimportant, but those desires, even the faint ones, are calling to us for a reason. They contain incredibly valuable messages that we need to hear if we are going to live authentically. How can we create our most authentic life if we aren't even willing to notice when our heart speaks? How can we do what we came into this life to do if we dismiss the desires of our heart as selfish, frivolous, unattainable or unnecessary? Our desires deserve our attention and our respect. If we ignore them, we are ignoring the truth of who we are and why we bothered to come into this world. This is not to say that every desire should be acted upon, but we owe it to our self to examine them, gain the information they hold for us, and then make conscious choices about how to proceed. When we fail to do that, we are doing our self a great disservice.

The Difference Between an Intention and a Goal

When it comes to setting intentions, it can be easy to confuse the "what" with the "why". You may be aware that you desire a certain thing, but your heart knows there is a deeper desire behind that desire. That deeper desire is the feeling you believe will come from obtaining that certain thing. For instance, maybe you notice that you long to take a vacation. To uncover the deeper reason behind your desire for a vacation, you ask yourself, "What will a vacation bring into my life?" Maybe it's relaxation, rejuvenation, and some much needed fun. Maybe it's the feeling of adventure or the excitement of a new experience. Or maybe, it's that feeling of connection with your family that you've been missing lately. The vacation is the "what" – the goal you wish to attain. The experience or the feeling the vacation will bring is the "why" – the desire behind the desire, or the intention.

As another example, let's say you have chosen to simplify just one room in your home by clearing out the physical clutter. Your "what" seems pretty obvious here. "I want my space to be less cluttered" or maybe "I want to use this room differently." There is most likely a deeper truth behind your desire to be uncovered. Why do you want your space to be less cluttered? How will you feel when your space is less cluttered? Maybe it's the feeling of freedom that you will experience when that space is cleared. Maybe it's the feeling of pride you will have when you have friends or family over. Maybe it's the feeling of peace you will feel when you come home to a beautiful, calm and clutter free space every night. When you can answer the "why" you become aware of your heart's true desire and why that goal is important. At that point you have set your clear and conscious intention.

A "what" without a "why" is fragile and can be easier to discard and ignore. Think of your goals as the support system of your intention. This will help you ground those goals in something much grander and deeper than any goal can be on its own. Now your goals are part of a bigger picture, a picture that serves as a reminder of what's really important to you. If your goal is not grounded in a clear and conscious intention, it can begin to feel like a grind at some point and that makes it much easier to walk away from it. When you are clear on your intention, your goals feel much less like a chore. It's the difference between drudgery (cleaning out your wardrobe) and a desire (creating a better start to the day for you and consequently, your family). Big difference!

ALIGNING YOUR INTENTION WITH YOUR VALUES

When we take the time to identify our "why", we bring awareness to the values that are driving our desire. Any intention will lack meaning if that intention is not in alignment with one or more of our values. For example, if your intention is to consciously simplify by clearing out the clutter in your kitchen so that your family can enjoy sharing meals together more, it's a fairly safe guess that you value connecting with your family. Setting your intention requires asking yourself "What value(s) of mine is this desire connected to?" When you know that your intention is in alignment with something you value, you are coming from a place of authenticity and the process will become much more meaningful for you. Something you formerly viewed as a big ol' pain in the butt might just become enjoyable for you when you are clear that your intention is in alignment with the things you hold most dear in life.

One Intention, Many Goals

It may take many goals to support your intention. For example, when we set the goal to write this book, it was to support our intention to share information that would empower others to simplify their life. Writing the book became the main goal that would support our intention, but we also had to set many other goals along the way. First, we set the goal of outlining everything we thought the book should include. Our next goal was to tweak that outline into a format that would be simple to read. Because we live in different cities and each have our own set of skills, we also had to set a goal of determining the best way to collaborate and co-write. Once we reached that goal, we set individual goals for creating the time within our respective schedules to write and review each other's work. And toward the end, we had to set weekly goals for the editing (ugh), and finally for publishing.

As you can see, there were multiple goals necessary to write this book, and each of those goals needed to be anchored to our intention of sharing empowering information. That anchor is what helped us focus on the very reason we were doing this in the first place. It allowed the process to stay meaningful for us as we moved forward and it certainly helped us during those times we felt stuck!

Staying Focused on What You Want

"Where attention goes, energy flows"

~ Denise Linn

One of the things we've both noticed in our coaching practices is that when we ask someone what they want, they almost always tell us what they don't want. Honestly, almost every time! "What do you want in a partner?" "Well, I don't want another cheater." "What do you want in a job?" "Well, I don't want that long commute." "What do you want in a new home?" "Well, I don't want to be by a noisy highway again." We can be so programmed to focus on the negative, that even when we think we are talking about what we want, we often are actually talking about what we don't want!

Whatever it is you want, a partner who is faithful, a short commute to work, a quiet setting for your new home, or anything else, take a look to make sure you are stating it and thinking of it in the positive. Whatever we focus on we give our energy to, and whatever we give our energy to will expand in our life. So, if you want a life that is simpler and allows you the time and energy to manifest the things and experiences that are important to you, make sure that is your focus, as opposed to the clutter or the time and energy drains you don't want anymore. This may seem like a small difference, but it makes all the difference in the world.

The good news is, if you're clear on what you don't want, it's relatively easy to identify what you do want by simply asking yourself a few questions. For example, if you are clear that you don't want to feel stressed out by the clutter in your bedroom anymore the question becomes, "What's the opposite of feeling stressed out by the clutter in my bedroom?" That question can lead you quite quickly to what it is you do want. Maybe the answer is that you want your bedroom to help you feel calm, peaceful and relaxed when you go to bed at night. Or, maybe you want your bedroom to feel like a sanctuary, a safe place where you can go to shut out the rest of the world. Maybe what you want is a bedroom that encourages your romantic and sensual side, or maybe you simply want to wake up every morning in a space that reminds you of how beautiful the world can be.

So when creating your intention, go ahead and identify what you don't want, but then move to and keep your focus firmly on what you do want. And remember that if we focus on what we don't want, we will see more of what we don't want in our life. If we keep our focus on what we do want, we will see more of what we do want in our life. It's that simple and it's that important.

S<small>TAYING</small> O<small>N</small> T<small>RACK WITH</small> I<small>NTENTION</small>

Even with a clear intention that aligns with our goals and values, we can be tested to stay on track. Sometimes we face a task that is very difficult, sometimes self-doubt creeps in, sometimes motivation is lacking. Whatever the reason, acknowledge the challenge for what it is, remind yourself why you began in the first place, and ask what you might do differently to support your effort. Maybe you need to take a break for a while, or you need to enlist other resources, or you just simply need to take smaller steps to reach the desired outcome. As we share with our following experiences, it can all be worth it.

T<small>ERESA'S</small> S<small>TORY</small>

My husband and I made the decision to sell our condo and purchase a home. A home that, although once beautiful, had been much neglected and was attached to an even more neglected and quite abused piece of property. It looked like a crazy move to many, I'm sure, but the moment I set eyes on it, my heart was calling me to restore this diamond in the rough back to its full potential and to create a peaceful, serene and joy-filled sanctuary for my husband and myself. A home where our grown sons, their significant others, and our future grandchildren could gather and enjoy for years to come. And so this became my intention.

Because my husband travels a great deal for work, and because this was actually my dream, I happily took on the bulk of the responsibility of creating the transformation. Starting with the house, I spent months organizing contractors, calling in favors from friends and family and doing much of the hands-on labor myself. (A girl can learn a whole lot about DIY home improvement on YouTube, by the way). It was possibly the biggest challenge I have ever taken on in my life, but it was a labor of love and intention and I am still giddy over the results.

As challenging as renovating the house was, when spring arrived and it was time to clean up and restore the property, I realized I had possibly bitten off more than I could chew. In addition to a large, overgrown and weed infested yard, there was a half-acre of wooded area with hidden sections of barbed wire that was massively overgrown with numerous dead trees and invasive vines, and had been used for a couple decades as a dumping ground for debris.

The words "it can't be done" crept into my thoughts more than once as I contemplated the clean-up, and I will admit to a couple mild panic attacks. But even as I talked myself down from the ledge, I couldn't ignore the calling of my heart to restore this once beautiful bit of nature back to its full glory. Deep down I knew that as I nurtured this disrespected, abused and neglected property back to health, something inside of me would also be transformed.

And so I set my intention to heal and restore the beauty of our little piece of nature and to create a sanctuary for myself, my family and my friends to enjoy, as well as a place for the birds, deer, chipmunks, and various other critters to thrive in. Of course I wanted the property to look nicer, but my "why" was much deeper than that, and when I became consciously aware of my "why", no amount of barbed wire, discarded tires or poison ivy was going to stop me.

No matter what my specific goal of the day was -- remove fallen branches, rake leaves, remove invasive vines, blaze trails, haul brush, spray poison ivy, plant flowers, hang bird feeders -- they all served to support my intention. Had I not stayed conscious of that intention, I doubt I would have had it in me to accomplish those goals and I doubt I would now be enjoying this beautiful space with my friends and family.

I listened to the callings of my heart and I discovered that my heart has a deep desire for beauty. I discovered that my heart desires the sanctity of a peaceful, healing space, a space where I can center myself and reconnect with my soul and with my family. And, I discovered that my spirit is nourished by time in nature. All of these desires were wrapped up in my clear intention and my intention was in alignment with some deeply held values. Because I had taken the time to listen to my heart's desires, set my intention in a positive manner and stay focused on that intention, I was able to hang on when I was up to my ears in discarded tires, rotting tree trunks and snake sightings. I was able to clear out what I didn't want in order to find myself surrounded by what I love and have consciously chosen.

Barbara's Story

When my husband, Gerry, died in October 2008, I embraced conventional wisdom and planned to stay in my home in Florida for a year before making any major decisions. Five weeks later I was laid off from my job and two weeks after that my son, who lived in Indianapolis, told me he was going to propose to his girlfriend. Quite suddenly, conventional wisdom didn't make sense anymore and I had a longing to move back home to Indianapolis. Only problem was the financial crisis, the Great Recession, that climaxed that fall. The area I lived in southwest Florida was one of the hardest hit real estate markets in the country. While it was not the best formula for selling a home, my intention was clear. I wanted to move back to Indianapolis where my family and life-long friends were located. That was my goal. My "why" was to be an active participant in my son and future daughter-in-law's wedding plans, as well as to surround myself with

45

the people who I knew would support me unconditionally as I moved into the next chapter of my life.

To say I put laser focus on the effort is an understatement. As I prepared my home for sale, I recognized I was competing with dozens of sellers in my community who needed to sell their homes because of the economic downturn. I also knew that there was very little I could do to bring potential buyers to my home other than to list the house with a trusted realtor and to pray. To support the part of my prayer to stay very clear on my intention, I created a vision board that represented what I wanted and why it was important to me. It included a picture of my Florida home with a "sold" sign in the yard, photos of the Indianapolis skyline and the specific area of town near friends and family I wanted to live and convenient to the services and areas I previously frequented. I posted pictures of the type of house and rooms I wanted along with the smiling faces of my family and friends. All of those pictures symbolized a very clear "why" I wanted to be back in Indianapolis.

Florida friends and neighbors were doubtful that I would be able to sell in a very depressed market and when I sensed they were about to make comments about those doubts or question me if I really thought I'd be able to sell, I stopped them before the first word. I thanked them for their concern and declared that the perfect buyers were on their way to purchase my home and would find the same joy in owning it that I did. While I tried hard to not allow anything that would negate my steadfast intention to sell my home and move to Indianapolis, I did wonder what would I do if my home didn't sell? How would I handle the disappointment of not being with my family and helping to plan my son's wedding? It was challenging to stay on track with my intention and I was grateful for the vision board and affirmations that I employed daily to keep me from the rabbit hole of negativity.

I listed my house in December 2008 and in March 2009 I received two offers close to my asking price. My home was one of the very few that sold in the neighborhood that winter, the highest selling season in that part of the country. In April I made the move back to Indianapolis. Months later after a temporary stay in an apartment before purchasing and moving into my permanent home, I was unpacking and found my vision board photos that sent chills throughout my body. I was living exactly in the area where I posted my intention. The house and room photos I put on the board were eerily similar to the home I bought. The universe understood my clarity and responded. I believe it was because my goal, my intention, and my values were in perfect alignment and unwavering. It was an extremely important lesson to me about the power of our thoughts and our intentions and my gratitude continues to this day.

SETTING YOUR INTENTION FOR CONSCIOUS SIMPLICITY

Let's take a look at what we now know about setting a clear intention for anything we desire.

- We know that we need to be ready *and* willing to take steps to create the life we want.
- We know how important it is to pay attention to the callings of our heart as we create our intentions.
- We know that our heart knows our "desire behind our desire" and that there is a difference between a goal – "what" we want, and an intention – "why" we want it.
- We know that our goals are meant to support our intentions.
- We know that our intentions must be in alignment with one or more of our values if they are going to serve us well.
- We know it may require many goals to fulfill one intention.
- We know it is important to stay focused on what we want, as opposed to what we don't want.
- We know that staying focused on our intention will help keep us on track when the going gets rough.

With those reminders in place, we invite you to get started setting your intentions. We have created a guide, Creating Your Intention Statement, in the Resources section to help you set your personal intention for creating more Conscious Simplicity in your life.

CHAPTER 5

FORGIVENESS, COMPASSION AND GRATITUDE

"Forgive others, not because they deserve forgiveness, but because you deserve peace."

~DESMOND TUTU

FORGIVENESS

IF WE ARE cluttering up our present life by holding onto grudges, disappointments, regrets or other hurts from the past, moving toward Conscious Simplicity will most likely require some forgiveness. There is a circular quality between forgiveness and letting go. Just as forgiveness can help us to let go, letting go often requires a healthy dose of forgiveness. When we forgive our self or someone else, we can let go of the guilt, the negative feelings, the regrets, and the "shoulds" we've held onto and that are keeping us stuck. When we forgive and release that emotional clutter, we also open the way to release physical clutter because the two are so frequently intertwined. One thing is clear, when we are in the process of releasing, it is important to keep a container of forgiveness nearby.

While holding onto a grudge, disappointment or regret certainly creates inner clutter, it's often also easy to see the connection between our lack of forgiveness and the outer clutter we are hold-ing onto. Maybe we are holding onto the clutter because we need to forgive our self for all the clothes we bought and never wore; for spending too much money on an item that brings no real value to our life; for allowing all this stuff to accumulate and clutter our spaces. Or maybe we need to forgive a family member for wast-ing money acquiring unneeded things. Perhaps it's forgiving the feelings that come up whenever we look at an item that has been difficult to release. And then other times, we aren't even aware of the connection between our inability to forgive, let go, and move our life forward because of anger, hurt, or disappointment. Such was the case with Katrina.

After nearly 25 years of marriage, Katrina was left shocked and reel-ing when her husband, Mitch, unexpectedly asked for a divorce. As the shock wore off and Katrina's sadness turned to anger, she vowed that she would make his life miserable. Her suspicion that there was another woman involved fueled Katrina's anger even more and she was deter-mined to "take him for everything he has." Katrina appeared to get what she wanted. Mitch didn't fight her for any of their possessions, including their house, furnishings, or vehicles. Their three children were grown and on their own, so child support was not an issue, but Mitch agreed to a hefty monthly spousal support payment and basically walked away with the clothes on his back. Still this was not enough for Katrina, who was determined to make him pay for what he did, and who was now letting her bitterness and resentment drive her actions. She held on tight to her anger, her victimhood and to anything and everything that had belonged to Mitch, even refusing to allow him to take his own set of golf clubs or the family heirlooms left to him when his parents passed away. It wasn't that she planned to sell them, pass them on to her children, or even to give them away. Her plan instead was to let them sit, unused and collecting dust in a barn at the back of her property, simply because she did not want Mitch to have them.

Those who knew Katrina were hopeful that as she worked through the wide range of emotions that come with a marital break-up or betrayal she would, for her own good, begin to come to terms with what had happened and to find a way to let go of her bitterness, as well as her need to hold onto possessions that were clearly serving no purpose in her life. Unfortunately, this did not happen. More than a decade since Mitch and Katrina divorced, it would be fair to say that Katrina's life remains stuck right where it was. She remains stuck in her anger and has grown even more bitter with the passing of years. She continues to badmouth Mitch to their grown children and to anyone else who will listen, straining several of her own relationships in the process. She lives in the same house she admits is far too big for one person, surrounded by the same things, many of which she doesn't particularly like but isn't willing to part with. And her barn is still filled with Mitch's personal, dust covered possessions that he long since let go. She is still working the same job, which brings her no pleasure and although she has expressed a desire to have a man in her life again, Katrina's attempts at dating have not gone well because, as it turns out, bitterness is a bit of a turn off. Go figure.

In the meantime, Mitch has moved on, repaired his relationship with his children despite Katrina's best efforts to the contrary, expanded his family business, fallen in love again and remarried, bought a new home and basically rebuilt his life. Both Mitch and Katrina had a choice to make when their marriage ended. One chose to move forward and one chose to stay stuck in the past. While Katrina's anger toward Mitch may have been justified, holding onto it has kept her own life stuck and unable to move forward, not his.

As Katrina's story demonstrates, forgiveness is not something we do for others, it is something we do for our self. That concept can best be summed up with the oft-quoted saying, "Holding a grudge is like drinking rat poison and waiting for the rat to die." When we don't forgive, we hold the toxins and contaminate our thinking and our being. When we fail to forgive, we hold our self in the energy of the past, but when we reach for forgiveness, we begin to release that energy and any hold it has on our life. Extending forgiveness can be extremely difficult and because of that it is actually a sign of strength, not of weakness.

Valerie's experience with her father demonstrates that the choice to forgive while not always an easy one, especially when we've been hurt by someone we love, can be done. It can also be very liberating, and it demonstrates once again, *it is something we do for our self.*

Valerie's relationship with her father had always been complicated. Her childhood was far from ideal and, at least in her eyes, contained enough examples of bad parenting to fill a book. As an adult, Valerie secretly carried resentment toward both of her parents, but especially toward her father for choosing to look the other way during the times her mother had both physically and emotionally abused her growing up. She had been possibly more hurt by her father's failure to protect her, than she was by her mother's abuse, and she carried that hurt into adulthood.

When Valerie's mother passed away and her father was diagnosed with cancer, Valerie stepped up to help him through his grieving process and cared for him through his own medical treatments. She felt closer to him than she had in her life and she was hopeful for the first time that things could be better between them. When his cancer went into remission and he no longer needed her daily assistance, Valerie was grateful for having been able to share that challenging time with her Father. But their new bond was short lived and their relationship fell apart when Valerie attempted to talk to her father about her painful childhood. Not only was he not willing to discuss the past, he stopped speaking to Valerie all together, leaving her hurt, confused and angry all at the same time.

Months went by with no contact between the two, despite a few attempts on Valerie's part, and she felt nearly devastated by his refusal to talk. Her feelings alternated between anger, sadness, disappointment, and relief at the thought of never having to try to make their relationship right again. More painful childhood memories came up and more resentment surfaced as Valerie tried to make sense of it all, and finally she vowed to never have contact with her father again. Still she was stuck in her anger and unable to move forward.

It was over a year later when Valerie's father reached out to her unexpectedly. She was at first shocked and then she was furious. Who the hell did he think he was reappearing in her life after refusing to speak to her for so long? Who the hell was he to put her through so much pain and then to think he could simply show back up again? Between his failure to protect her as a child, his refusal to hear how painful that had been for her, and his previous refusal to speak to her, Valerie's first instinct was to hang on tight to her anger, walk away and never look back. She may have been justified in doing so. But that is not what she chose.

Valerie's decision to forgive her father was not instantaneous, but it was just that, a decision. It was a choice that felt better to her than staying angry, hurt, shut down and resentful, and it was a choice she made consciously. Valerie chose to forgive her father's shortcomings as a parent, as well as his inability to talk with her about her painful childhood, and even his most recent behavior. She made this choice because, more than anything she wanted to be free of the past and free of her anger. Consciously choosing forgiveness is what finally brought Valerie the freedom she had been seeking. No doubt, her childhood had not been perfect, her father was not perfect, and their relationship was probably never going to be perfect either, but hanging onto her anger was not going to change any of that. When Valerie chose forgiveness, she did not *find perfection, but she did find peace of mind and the freedom to move her life forward.*

WHAT DOES FORGIVENESS MEAN?

I (Teresa) admit that the word "forgiveness" brings up a lot of conflicted feelings for me. As a matter of fact, I've noticed that every time I decide to sit down and write about forgiveness, I instead convince myself that I'm starving and must eat immediately or will lapse into a hunger induced coma. Before writing this, I polished off two helpings of leftover mashed potatoes and three red, white and blue popsicles in an attempt to postpone delving into this topic. Clearly, food is my favorite form of avoidance, but since my belly was full and I was out of popsicles, the time had come to take a look at what I've been avoiding.

Here is what I know. I'm not even particularly fond of the word forgiveness. I find myself throwing up mental blocks whenever I hear it. Not because I don't believe in it, but because it tends to conjure up all kinds of lofty expectations for me. Expectations that, frankly, I'm not sure I could ever live up to. So, what I am proposing here is that if the word forgiveness triggers anything negative inside of you, just feel free to call it something else. I prefer to simply think of it as letting go, or releasing the past, or moving forward. That feels best to me. Choose whatever term or words feel best to you if it helps because, whatever you call it, forgiveness really will change your life.

It's important to mention that forgiveness does not mean we condone the actions or behaviors of the person we are forgiving, or that we are willing to let history repeat itself, or even that we necessarily allow someone back into our life. What forgiveness does mean is that we are ready to move out of the energy of the past and release the hold it has on us. We are no longer willing to allow our self to be angry, sad, hurt, shut down or controlled by something or someone from our past. We are taking back the power we gave away to the person, to the situation, or to the experience that we have been unable to forgive. We are moving our life forward at the same time we are setting healthy boundaries for our self and sticking to them.

Another thing I realized (somewhere between the second and third popsicle) is that some of my conflict comes from not having a clear definition of what forgiveness is. As much as I may believe that forgiveness is a good thing, and as much as I may want to consider myself a forgiving person, the truth is that it has all just seemed like a very vague and complicated concept to me.

I have wondered if I'm even capable of true forgiveness, or by whose standards I should be forgiving, for that matter. I knew I needed to simplify the concept of forgiveness in my own mind and to find a definition that fully resonated with me. After all, it's pretty tough to hit the mark of forgiveness if you aren't clear on what you're aiming for. Further, I needed to define it in a way that felt good to me, rather than to continue to see it as some unattainable concept that only the holiest of saints could ever pull off, because I hate it when I set up myself up for failure.

So, I have created a definition of forgiveness that feels simple and right to me. I invite you to adopt it too, if you like it, or to find another one that resonates with you because that clarity will be needed as you move forward. I do know that forgiveness is an act of self-love and while it will not change your past, it will change your future. Forgiving others will not necessarily change who they are, but it will change who you are and, it will absolutely get your life out of stuck mode in ways you can barely imagine. Forgiveness may not be easy, but it is clearly a choice

worth making. With that in mind, here is my personal definition of forgiveness.

*Forgiveness means: I choose to stand in my power by releasing any hold
the unchangeable past has on me.*

*Forgiveness means: I choose to no longer give any of my energy away to
the wrongs I believe have been committed against me in the past.*

*Forgiveness means: I choose to let nothing from the past stand in the
way of the life I want now.*

*Forgiveness means: I choose to take full responsibility for my own hap-
piness from this moment forward.*

*Forgiveness means: I choose to release any thoughts, beliefs or actions
that get between me and my peace of mind.*

Forgiveness means: I choose to live my life with an open heart.

Forgiveness is a choice. And like other choices in life, some
are easy while others are more difficult. Recognize it may take
time to reach a state of forgiveness in some situations. When you
notice the anger, the hurt, or the resentment creeping back in,
reaffirm what forgiveness means to you and why it is so important.
Reaffirm your intention to simplify your life by letting go of that
which does not serve you.

Unconditional Forgiveness

If we attach conditions to forgiveness, such as requiring an admis-
sion of guilt, an apology, or the making of amends, we may be
setting our self up to never be free of our anger, hurt or disappointment. For a variety of reasons, we may never get the apology
or acknowledgment of guilt we think we deserve, and sometimes a
wrong can simply not be made right. Obviously this is true when the
person or persons we need to forgive has passed on. Other times
the offender simply may not be capable of accepting responsibility

for what he or she has done, and in some cases, may not even be aware that their actions have caused us pain. If we hang onto our pain until our conditions are met, we may be sentencing our self to a lifetime of grudge clutter. And when we bring the energy of past hurts into our present moments, we are pretty much guaranteeing that history will repeat itself, one way or another. So, we invite you to consider unconditional forgiveness as an act of kindness to yourself.

Remember, choosing to forgive or let it go is not for them. It's for us. And, while we may initially need some time to talk through and process what has happened with someone we trust, we need to stay very conscious of not getting stuck in it. There comes a point when, if we continue to talk about it, think about it, focus on it, re-live it, seek revenge for it, or use it as an excuse to hold our self back or keep our hearts guarded, we give our energy and our power away to it.

Let's face it, if we are human someone will, at some point in our life, offend us, hurt us, disappoint us, or break our heart. We can choose to stay stuck in our pain until our conditions are met, or we can let it go, step into our own power, and move on to creating the life we want and deserve. When we make the choice to unconditionally remove our energy from the pain of the past and let it go, we free up the space for more happiness, joy, success, love and fun in our life.

FORGIVING FROM A DISTANCE

Forgiveness does not mean we are required to put our self in harm's way or allow someone who is toxic to be a part of our life. Sometimes it's necessary to forgive from a distance. If we do not feel emotionally or physically safe with someone, or if we find that they are consistently a drain on our energy, releasing them from our life may be the only answer. In those instances, we can make the choice to simply let them go, both literally and energetically. We can wish them well as we wish them away. In cases where it's not possible to let them go from our physical presence, for example, a toxic co-worker, we can at least energetically distance our self from them by making the choice to give their negative behavior as little of our focus as humanly possible. Forgiveness doesn't even necessarily require a conversation with the person we are forgiving. It's simply the choice we make to no longer give any of our energy or peace of mind away to them.

Forgiving Our Self

Sometimes the hardest person to forgive is our self. If we are human, we have done things in our life that we regret and most of us are really good at beating our self up over them, often on a long-term basis. I (Teresa) have made choices in life I would not make again, and I know that I have caused pain to others in the course of my lifetime, usually unintentionally, but pain nonetheless, and I have struggled to forgive myself for those times. Among the things I have struggled with forgiving myself for are the times that I have betrayed myself by not being authentic. They are the times that I didn't stand up for what felt right to me, didn't speak my truth and/or went along with something that my gut was telling me was wrong. But what I know is this, if we allow our self to wallow in the energy of our past mistakes and regrets, we rob our self and others of the opportunity to experience the best of who we are. Of course, learning what we can from the experience and making amends whenever possible is always a good start. But from there, we need to accept that mistakes are a part of being alive and simply choose to let it go so that we can focus on who we want to be now, in this present moment. When we make the conscious choice to forgive our self and release the past, we are freeing up space in our life to become our best self, and once again, to move our life forward.

COMPASSION AND GRATITUDE

"The miracle of gratitude is that it shifts your perception to such an extent that it changes the world you see."

~ DR. ROBERT HOLDEN

The quickest ways to forgiveness are through compassion and gratitude. With compassion we realize we aren't the only one who makes mistakes. We recognize that our story isn't unique; there is a shared experience for whatever misery or misfortune we think we alone have endured. And we are reminded that mistakes are easily made when we are coming from a place of fear. With compassion we recognize also that those who have offended us acted out of their own fears, their own insecurities, their own humanness. When we live with compassion, we open our self to greater understanding and ability to forgive.

When we take the time to be consciously grateful, we can change our perspective on almost anything. Being grateful puts us in a state of peace, contentment and openness, which is a great state of mind to be in if you have some forgiving to do. Gratitude helps us remember that within every challenge, difficulty or painful situation is a gift. Granted, it can be tough to see the gift in the midst of the fear, anger or pain we are experiencing. But when we recognize and focus on gratitude for the gift the situation brought forth, whether it is new insights, lessons learned, or strengths developed, we are able to move our life forward. And as we receive the gift, it is easier to extend forgiveness.

Consider starting a gratitude journal if you haven't already. Each day write down three to five things you are grateful for before you go to sleep or start your day without repeating any items. It seems pretty simple, but writing your gratitude journal on a bad day can be challenging. Several weeks into the exercise, you can be struggling to come up with new entries for which you are grateful. And that's where you dig deep. That's where you discover the little things you are grateful for that previously were overlooked, and where you might start looking at people and situations in your life a little differently. In the Resources section, we have provided some statements of gratitude you may find helpful.

Setting an Intention for Forgiveness

"There comes a day when you realize turning the page is the best feeling in the world, because there is so much more to the book than the page you were stuck on."

~ Zayn Malik

If there's a regret, grievance, hurt, disappointment, anger or any other "grudge clutter" you would like to release, setting a clear intention will go a long way to help you stay focused and let go. When you are clear about what you want to release and why, you will be much better prepared to move forward in the releasing process. With that in mind, we have prepared a tool to help you create your intention for forgiveness that is provided in the Resources section. Start small if you need to, and be honest with yourself about what you are feeling. Don't worry about doing this right. This is no time to strive for perfection. Actually, there is *no* time to strive for perfection! Just trust that you will find your way and be kind to yourself as you go.

CHAPTER 6

RELEASING PHYSICAL CLUTTER

"The ability to simplify means to eliminate the unnecessary
so the necessary may speak."

~ HANS HOFFMAN

JUST AS OUR bodies are containers for food and our brains are containers for thought, our homes and other spaces are containers for our physical possessions. What we allow in our bodies, our brains, our homes and other spaces has an effect on our physical, mental, spiritual and emotional energies. When we stay conscious of what we put into our containers, we are consciously creating our life rather than living it by default. When we make the choice to consciously release the physical clutter in our life, we begin to see our life shift, not only on the physical level, but on mental, emotional and spiritual levels too. Consciously releasing the unimportant physical stuff from our life, the stuff we no longer need, love or enjoy, is an empowering statement to the Universe that we are ready to make room in our life for what is important to us. Let's take a look at some ways we can prepare our self for the actual process of letting go.

THE PREPARATION

Remember to focus on the goal and intention for your space. As we discussed in Chapter Four, creating an intention of what we *do* want and why it is important is one of the first steps to releasing what no longer serves us. By getting clear about what we want, it becomes easier to let go of anything that doesn't support that intention. Beginning the releasing process with the right frame of mind is also crucial. If you're feeling ambivalent, you will second-guess your decisions. And indecision leads to inaction.

I (Barbara) am reminded of the countless times I've been in my closet selecting clothes for the day when I see items that I need to donate. I'm unwavering in my thought but unfortunately, I don't have time to do anything about it at that moment. I've returned to the closet later to discover I'm no longer as definite as I was earlier. For some reason, I think perhaps I would wear that piece of clothing again, or I remember how much I enjoyed wearing it when I lived in a tropical climate and my lifestyle was different. Because I get caught up with my attachment to the item and what it once was for me, it remains on the hanger. Only when I renew my intention and focus on what I want now in my life and what I love and use now in my life, and sometimes even enlist the help of a friend, am I able to move the seldom or never worn clothing and donate it to a charity.

Always be willing to look at the deeper meaning you have attached to the items as you go. And remember, we are not talking about getting rid of everything! This is about releasing the things that don't represent who you are *now* or the life you want to create for yourself *now*. Our life constantly changes as we grow, evolve and expand. It stands to reason that the things we surround our self with would naturally change too.

Stay conscious of your self-talk. This is equally important as you prepare and as you go through the process of releasing the clutter. What are you telling yourself as you head into this process? Are your thoughts encouraging or have you convinced yourself that this has to be a big pain? What thoughts show up consistently as you go through your stuff? Pay attention to the answers as they often contain valuable information about whether to keep something or let it go. If you hear yourself thinking, "This makes me sad," ask yourself if it makes sense to keep the sadness around. How does it support you? If you are telling yourself that you would feel too guilty letting something go, ask yourself where that guilt might be coming from, how it is serving you and whether it might be time to let that guilt go too. Or if "what a mess" surfaces, ask yourself what would it be like to create a calmer, more organized environment for yourself. What would it be like to think "this is so calming" rather than "what a mess" every time you walk into the room? It might also help to examine if a dose of forgiveness is in order, either for yourself or someone else.

Consciously affirming what you want to experience during the releasing process can serve as a supportive reminder too. It's not always easy to let go of our things. Affirming that "I move through this process with joy and ease" and "I am kind to myself in this process" can help tremendously in shifting negative thoughts or self-talk.

Be willing to shift perspectives. Neuroscience research has shown that you cannot create positive change from a negative attitude. What motivation that is to practice changing perspectives! When we change our perspective about something, we change the energy of it. We also change the energy within us. How do we do that? First, we commit a willingness to see our stuff differently.

We define a clear intention of what we want to create and why it's important, and we choose to see our stuff in the context of that intention, rather than separate from it. Secondly, we choose to stay aware of what we allow into our home, our space, our thoughts, and our life and the effect it has on our physical, mental and emotional energies. Again, this is a choice!

I (Barbara) love affirmations. When I'm feeling out of sorts or notice that my thoughts are veering off the intended target, an affirmation brings me back to center. I won't pretend it doesn't take repeated efforts, most times it does. The words can be just words until I focus quiet, mindful attention on what I'm saying. And then I notice that my perspective begins to shift away from the negative to a more positive attitude.

Consider practicing the use of affirmations to see how they work for you. We've prepared a worksheet with some simple affirmations in the Resources section that might be helpful as you work to shift your perspective.

Reach for forgiveness, compassion, and gratitude before you even begin. Because our physical stuff is so often intricately connected to our mental and emotional stuff, it's most likely that the need for forgiveness, compassion and gratitude will come up. Setting out to be forgiving, compassionate and grateful to others, our circumstances and our self will create a state of mind that will allow the releasing process to flow. Remember, even as you are letting go of your stuff, you can acknowledge your gratitude for it. Maybe you once loved it. Maybe it once served you well, or maybe it was a gift from someone who loves you. Those are all things to be grateful for. Move into that place of gratitude for what you are now willing to release and remember that releasing it does not negate your gratitude for the purpose it once served in your life. Further, remember to acknowledge your gratitude for what you are moving towards. Again, affirmations can be helpful!

Accept what you are unable to change. Let's face it, there are times when releasing certain physical clutter from your life is beyond your control for the moment. Maybe you have a tattered sofa that lowers your energy every time you see it sitting smack in the middle of your living room, but are unable to afford a new one quite yet. Maybe you live with someone who won't budge with his or her own clutter, or perhaps you are even living in someone else's space. While we encourage you to release the unwanted clutter in your life whenever you possibly can, when doing so is simply not yet possible, we suggest it can be a perfect time to practice acceptance, and perhaps even forgiveness. What is important is to avoid any additional drain on your energy by focusing on what you can't change. Put your focus and your energy into what is actually within your control and move on. And, if it holds difficult or negative memories, but you have to live with it, consider intentionally changing the energy of it by performing your own energy shifting ritual as discussed in Chapter Three.

Preparing the intention, being mindful of the self-talk, shifting the perspectives, extending forgiveness, practicing compassion and gratitude, and accepting what you cannot change are critical precursors to support the mindset of Conscious Simplicity, but they won't perform the actual work of releasing. For that we need a process. A systematic, nuts and bolts process to keep us on task and help us release the clutter and create the environment we want. We've talked a lot about what keeps us stuck, now let's look at how to take action once we decide to embrace Conscious Simplicity.

THE PROCESS

Because we are unique individuals with our own set of values and needs, how we embrace and create Conscious Simplicity needs to be individual and unique to each of us. However, there is a logical method to follow that will help you experience success in the physical de-cluttering effort. Many professional organizers will say it many different ways, but the basic concept is the same. When I (Barbara) started my company I decided to use a part of my company name, Divine Order, to create an acronym for the process and make it easy to remember:

Organize
Reuse, reduce, recycle
Designate
Establish
Re-evaluate

Organize by category. And you get to decide what the category is. You can sort by color, by size, by use, by season, by person, by whatever way makes sense to you and is appropriate for the types of items you are organizing.

Reuse, reduce, recycle. As you sort, determine if you will keep (reuse); toss or shred (reduce); or donate, sell, or consign (recycle) your stuff. Save time and effort by placing items in a labeled bag, box, pile etc. as you go along. I highly recommend moving the stuff out as you progress. Keeping your donation bags until the project is finished will add to the visual clutter, and it may prompt temptation to retrieve items you've already decided to donate!

Designate a home and containerize. Once you know what you're keeping, figure out the best place to keep it. Think about how often you will use the item and where you will use it to determine the optimal storage location. Consider the concept of prime real estate – location, location, location! The things you use most often should be easy to access and put away. Place items in appropriate containers to facilitate the ease of use and to increase the likelihood they will stay neatly in place.

Establish a maintenance routine. If your things are maintained on a regular basis, they will be manageable. And if they are manageable, they will be easily maintained. Set up a rotating schedule so you are not faced with purging files, closets, toys, and cabinets all at the same time.

Re-evaluate your systems periodically. Recognize that life situations change and what worked previously may not work now, and what works well now may not be relevant at some point in the future. Be willing to adjust to accommodate your current situation.

Simple steps, yes. Challenging to accomplish, possibly. Beyond the basic steps of the organizing process outlined above there are many reminders and tools that also will support your successful effort. Let's look at some of the most critical to consider when engaged in a de-cluttering project.

Take small steps. Overwhelm is one of the primary reasons people don't reduce the clutter and organize. Clients frequently declare, "I am so overwhelmed. I don't know where to begin." When you're looking at an entire room or house or office, it can be very overwhelming. But because you've done the work to define your goals and intentions and you have a better understanding about the attachment to your stuff, you *are* ready to take those first steps. It's time to put the blinders on and focus on one area, one shelf, one drawer, or whatever seems manageable. What's important is to break the project into small tasks and take one step at a time. And remember that if you're having difficulty getting started, the first step is too big. Make it smaller. Even small steps will move you closer to your goal and allow you to celebrate successes along the way. It will move the feeling of overwhelm to a belief that it is doable, as experienced by one of Barbara's clients.

I (Barbara) completed an Assessment and developed an Action Plan for Jeanette, who wanted to de-clutter several areas in her home. She embraced the small step philosophy and carved out small segments of time in her very busy work and home schedule in order to organize. She set up account-ability to help stay on track by sending me an email each week with updates on how much time she spent working in various areas of her home. Very brief emails would report things such as, "two 20-minutes sessions sorting through papers," "one 45-minute session cleaning out kitchen drawer," or "worked three 30-minute days and one 15-minute day."

When Jeanette shared in one of her messages that she felt she wasn't making very much progress, I sent her a reply with the cumulative hours she spent. She was surprised to see how the time had added up and summed it up with "slow and steady."

We continued with the email exchange for many months as she found checking in with me provided some accountability for her. The tone of her messages gradually changed as she realized how the small steps moved her to her goal without creating additional stress on her limited available time. As she became more aware of the noticeable changes she was making, she felt encouraged and reported, "It spurs me on!"

This isn't to say that all de-cluttering projects will take weeks or months to complete, but if you can only devote a small amount of time at a time, take heart in knowing it can be done!

It's also important to understand that releasing the clutter is a *process* and not an event. And trust that there likely will be chaos before the calm. Things very well might feel and look worse before they feel and look better. The sorting process takes time and can require space until final "homes" are found for your stuff.

Recognizing that the clutter wasn't created overnight and won't be transformed overnight is probably not news. But it is essential to keep in mind to avoid frustration and fatigue.

Choose your starting point. There are many ways to approach the start of a de-cluttering effort and again, what's important is what works best for you. Tackling the areas of "low-hanging fruit" can help create confidence and a rhythm for releasing. For example, it may be an extra closet filled with clothes no longer worn, or a kitchen drawer of seldom used or duplicate utensils. Maybe it's a linen closet with worn sheets and towels. Pick an area you know won't hold much emotional attachment, and that will be easy to sort and decide. That can give you the momentum and confidence to keep the effort going.

Perhaps you prefer to start with the most challenging area first just to get it out of the way or because you know that it drains your energy every time you see it. Knowing that you have conquered the difficult can make the rest of the project seem less daunting. Or it might be more important to tackle the item or area that will give the biggest visual impact. The one that you can look at and say, "Wow. I did that and it feels and looks great!"

If a hundred choices are churning in your head, it might make sense to make a list and pick one based on your mood and time available that particular day. It's a good way to experience the freedom of choice. And if spontaneity and surprise motivate you, write all your tasks on separate note cards or post-its and randomly draw one before you begin the organizing effort. No one has to know if you don't like what you picked and you throw it back for a different selection!

Set aside a certain amount of uninterrupted time. Once you have set your intention and chosen a place to start, decide how long you want to work on a particular morning, afternoon or evening.

Whether it's 30 minutes, an hour, or 4 hours, be sure you are devoting the allotted time solely for the task at hand. This will go a long way to help you avoid being pulled away to answer e-mails, make phone calls, or get to the gym. If you're unsure how long you can give devoted attention, start with a specific increment of time, say 30 minutes, and set a timer. When the timer rings, notice how you're doing and how you feel. If you're still feeling energized set it for another time increment. Doing this for a period of work sessions will give you a good indication of your optimal work session length as well your optimal energy times of the day.

Pay attention to your energy levels while you work. If you start to feel tired or drained, it could be time to stop, or maybe take a break. Just be honest with yourself that you're not looking for an excuse to quit! Recognize that de-cluttering takes physical, mental and emotional energy. You will get tired.

Forget about doing it "right". Another often heard comment is "I don't know the right way to do it." There is a plethora of organizing books that can be rather unyielding in their direction about how to get organized. Certainly there are the basic concepts to follow to create ORDER that we discussed, but rarely is there one right way to do each of the steps. The right way is the way that works best for you. Clients are frequently surprised and often empowered when they realize they don't have to follow certain dictates to achieve their goal.

Ask for the help you need. Enlist a relative, friend or professional to join you in your effort. Partnering with objective, non-judgmental and supportive people can help tremendously, especially in letting go of the things that hold emotional, yet non-useful attachment. And it can make the process a lot more fun!

My (Barbara) closet was in dire need of pruning. I had moved from Florida to the Midwest and had clothes appropriate for both places. Yet each time I attempted to purge my wardrobe, I would get stuck as I thought, "I really like that top. I know I haven't worn it and it looks like something from Florida, but I'm sure I'll have an opportunity to wear it again." Or, "I'm sure the next time I go shopping I'll find something to wear with this," and, "This would be perfect to wear to a dressy affair," even though I long since stopped going to them.

About that time a dear friend and colleague, Susan, came to visit from out of state. One evening during her stay, I handed her a glass of wine and announced, "We're going to my closet!" For the next three hours, Susan's unbiased opinion, supportive approach, and gentle humor helped me fill three large trash bags of clothing for a local charity. It was wonderfully freeing as she helped me detach from my perceptions and offered insight about what she observed. We had many revelations and laughs going through the process that evening, and the experience with Susan has remained a special memory of our friendship.

Having a trusted partner work with you also allows an opportunity to talk about an item before you let it go. Countless times, I listen to clients recall the origin of an item or a memory attached to it. The simple act of being heard is often all they need to let the item go. Ask for the support you need.

Be willing to challenge and let go of your "old story." When your self-limiting thoughts rear their ugly heads, recognize them for what they are, an old story you have told yourself. Then be willing to challenge that old story and to let it go. Go ahead and acknowledge those thoughts, but know you have the option to simply push the "delete" button in your mind and replace them with new thoughts that actually support you. Know that you have the option to tell yourself a new story. If your old story was, "I can't let go of this stuff that I don't use or need anymore because it's a part of my past," ask yourself if that is really true and if that old story is serving you well. If it isn't, let it go and create a new story that serves you better. Perhaps, "I lovingly honor my past as I release these possessions and move my life forward." Repeating your new story as many times as necessary as you go through this process will help you stay focused on what you are creating at this moment in your life, rather than what you are leaving behind.

Set up accountability. For many people, some type of account-ability system is extremely helpful. It's not intended for reward or punishment, rather it's a tool to help stay on track. It doesn't need to be complicated or elaborate. A supportive friend or relative with whom you can check-in, much like Jeanette, who I mentioned earlier, who sent a weekly email. She didn't require that I respond but did ask if I didn't hear from her by Wednesday afternoon of each week, to please send an email asking how things were going. Another cli-ent chose to send a weekly text advising if she completed the tasks she committed to do. The thing about accountability is you get to decide what works for you and how best to set it up to make it effective.

Stay mindful. As you go along the releasing process, check in with yourself. How am I doing? What is coming up for me? Don't judge yourself. Just notice and employ any self-care techniques that may be helpful, especially if you experience emotional reac-tions. This is about self-awareness, not self-sabotage. If emotional stuff starts to surface in this process, take the time to consciously look a little deeper at what's really going on. Ask yourself what's behind the fear, anxiety or sadness you are experiencing, what memories are being triggered for you, and what is it you are really finding hard to release at the moment. Often difficult emotions surface when they are ready to be healed. Taking the time to jour-nal can be a good option to help you understand what is coming up for you, too.

Be sure to get the voices in your head to work as a team. It's not unusual to play ping-pong in your mind during the releasing process. You decide to donate an item. As you start to place it in a bag, a "maybe" or a "should" pops up. Your thoughts banter back and forth as you decide what to do and the "maybes" and "shoulds" become vague distractions that sidetrack the effort. ("*Maybe* I *should* keep this for a little while more" is one of my favorites!). Let "maybe" and "should" serve as red flags that something other than *your* truth is in play. Bring those conflicting voices mindfully back to the intention and the goal. And if doing that means you keep the item, that's great! What is important is that you keep or discard/donate something for the right reasons. The reasons that support your goal and intention, not disrupt them.

Don't be afraid to strike while the iron is hot. Planning is great, but if the urge to purge happens to take you by surprise, just go for it. There's no need to wait for the perfect time or circumstances. If the mood hits, jump right on in! One of Teresa's most productive clutter clearing experiences came as a complete surprise to her.

In the weeks following the women's group meeting, I was very mindful and deliberate about going through the closets, cupboards and drawers in my home in a systematic manner and was quite proud of the progress I had made. The one area I managed to avoid clearing though was my own clothes closet. Actually it would be more accurate to say my clothes "closets" since the master bedroom had two very spacious closets in it and I had claimed them both. Because they were so large and the previous owner had decked them out with all kinds of great shelving and other organizing gadgets, they looked very neat and tidy. For that reason, I saw no reason to bother going through them. Until one evening, that is.

I don't remember what prompted my closet clearing frenzy that night. I'm pretty sure I had only opened one of the closet doors to put away a pair of shoes when the urge struck. What I do remember though is once I got started, there was no stopping me. I had no idea the crazy amount of clothes I had managed to stuff into those closets. I pulled out every single item of clothing and piled them all on my bed, vowing to put back only the items I loved and actually wore. What followed were three hours of arguing with myself over what to keep and what to release. Many times I threw a blouse or pair of jeans in the donate pile, pulled them back out again, tried them on, beat myself up over ever having bought them in the first place, and then tried to convince myself I would wear them someday, only to eventually end up throwing them back in the donate pile. It wasn't pretty, but I was on a roll.

In the end, I lay exhausted on my bed, staring down at the gigantic heaps of clothing on my bedroom floor. Some of it was quite ugly, in my opinion. Some of it was okay, but just didn't fit properly, and some of it was just not my style. I poured myself a glass of Chardonnay and sat wondering what the heck I could have been thinking when I purchased most of it. As mortified as I was by what I saw, I forced myself to snap a couple of pictures and texted them to Barbara, who immediately called me laughing harder than I've ever heard her laugh. I told her I just needed someone to bear witness to my major accomplishment and we laughed some more at the irony of it all. When we hung up, I bagged everything up (into no less than five, 30-gallon garbage bags) and immediately hauled them out to my car. I wanted those clothes out of my sight as soon as possible, partly because I was afraid I might change my mind. These clothes served no purpose in my life. I didn't like them and I didn't wear them. Yet I had allowed them to take up space in my home. Worse yet, I had allowed them to take up my precious energy as I weeded through them every morning to get to the clothes I actually did wear. What a way to start my days!

My spontaneous, one-woman clothes purging party seemed to come out of nowhere that night, but I was glad I followed the urge. I was also pleasantly surprised by how good it felt to have those items out of my life. I hoped they would be of value to someone else, someone who would actually wear them, and I vowed to be much more conscious with clothes shopping moving forward. In this instance, I did no planning and I had no strategy. I just jumped into the monster of a job with very little thought. I'm not recommending that you wait until you are spontaneously inspired to tackle your clutter clearing, but sometimes it does happen that way.

Have some fun along the way. Regardless how you tackle the project, make it fun. Put on some music, sing to yourself, keep the vision of what you desire nearby, and schedule breaks and rewards along the way. And remember that you are seeking peace, not perfection!

Even with an understanding of the "nuts and bolts" of releasing, we can still get stuck when it comes to letting go of things we don't need anymore. Remember Barbara's clothes closet experience? For those times, there are questions we can ask our self to determine whether to keep or let go. We've provided a tool, Helpful Questions for the Release of Clutter Energy, in the Resources section so you can ask these questions yourself or have a supportive friend ask when you're stuck.

When It's Really Hard

> *"Be a ruthless editor of what you allow into your home.*
> *Ask yourself 'what does this mean to me'?"*
>
> ~ Nate Berkus

Embracing Conscious Simplicity requires releasing things that no longer bring value to us, but what if that thing holds some type of deeper or more complicated significance? What if we don't care for the item but have attachment to the person, identity, or experience it represents? How do we release the Jello molds, the glass pitcher, the decades of accumulated school papers?

For starters, stay in gratitude. At one time the item did serve a purpose for which thanks can be expressed. Assuming it will be donated or sold, be grateful that the item will find a new home and fulfill a need for someone else as it once did for you. Appreciate the fact that letting the item go opens the flow of energy for new things to come to you. Give thanks that you will always have enough.

From a place of gratitude, you can engage in a ritual to honor the items you are releasing. The ritual can be as simple as expressing a thank you, taking a picture of the item, or sharing your story about the item with someone else.

(BARBARA'S STORY)
My husband, Gerry, and I had different decorating tastes. He rarely involved himself in acquiring items for our home but when he did, I knew it was something he liked very much. One day he came home quite excited about silk orchids a local store was selling, and wanted me to go back with him to pick one out. He was certain I would love them. My outward agreement to go was matched by my inward reluctance, but I knew he really liked them and I acknowledged that he was doing something nice for me.

The orchid plants did nothing for me but we picked one out and it was placed on an entryway table in our home. After my husband died I packed the orchid (with the Jello molds!) and moved them from Florida to Indiana. The orchid claimed its space once again in the entryway until one day I looked at it from across the room and thought, "I really don't like that." The guilt was immediate and I was uncertain what to do.

I decided to remove the plant from the entry table and placed it on a shelf in my closet where it stayed for a few months. When I made the seasonal switch of clothes in my closet I came across the orchid again and knew I needed to do something with it but didn't know what that was. After pondering a few minutes, I heard myself say out loud, "I love you and I love your thoughtfulness in buying this for me. Getting rid of this orchid changes none of that. And it doesn't represent anything more than something you bought for me. This no longer fits my décor and I'm grateful I can donate this to someone who will enjoy it much more than I do. Thank you." That small act, a ritual of sorts, made it painlessly easy to let the orchid go without guilt. And to this day, I remember the love with which it was brought into my home and the love that allowed it to leave. I was grateful.

Sometimes there are many items and it can be difficult to just toss them all. Remember Debra and all her school teacher's paraphernalia that she believed defined who she was. We suggested to her that she pick a few very special items and display them. We reminded her that if everything is special, nothing is special. If our special stuff is stowed away, it really isn't very special, and it certainly isn't enjoyed. The same can be done with collections or memorabilia from a loved one who has passed on. Select a few things that hold exceptional significance and create an altar, a shelf, or a shadow box where they can be seen. And if it's not practical or appropriate to display, consider a decorative memory box to hold the items. Or take pictures of treasured items and place in a scrapbook, a digital file or photo album.

Brenda had to endure the unthinkable after her daughter, Jamie, died in a car accident. A year after experiencing the shock of losing her only daughter, and still very much in the process of grieving, a move to a smaller home forced Brenda to make some tough decisions about which of Jamie's possessions to keep and which to let go. Even under normal circumstances, Brenda considered herself to be quite a sentimental person. Her own Mother had died unexpectedly when Brenda was just fourteen, and she had felt comforted throughout her life by surrounding herself with some of her mother's possessions, as well as some passed down from her late grandparents. Letting go of items belonging to her deceased loved ones seemed like a betrayal and she wasn't sure she was at all up for letting go of anything that had belonged to her beloved Jamie. Fortunately, Brenda had a strong support system and with the help of friends and family she found her way through the process one step at a time. The process was painful at times, but at the same time healing for Brenda. Working through the sadness and guilt that came up with each item she released, Brenda's turning point came when she realized that her love for Jamie was not measured by the amount of Jamie's stuff she held onto. In the end, she chose to keep Jamie's scrapbooks, some of her fabric and other sewing notions because both Mom and daughter were gifted seamstresses, and a few other items with special meaning. In addition, a kind neighbor offered to make Brenda a special quilt from some of Jamie's favorite clothes, a gesture that warmed Brenda's heart and made it easier for her to let the other things go.

While releasing the possessions of our deceased loved ones can be one of the most difficult things we ever do, it can also be an important part of the grieving process. Loving someone who has passed does not require holding onto all of their stuff, especially when that stuff keeps us stuck in our pain. Keeping a few significant items that can be seen and enjoyed go a long way toward keeping the memory and love alive.

Much like Barbara's reaction to the silk orchids from her husband and Teresa's thoughts about the glassware from her sons, we can get tripped up with gifts from others. Many of us have difficulty parting with items we no longer want or need simply because it was a gift from someone. If it's someone we're not particularly fond of, the tossing may not be so hard. But usually that's not the case. Here is a question for you – What is your intention when you give a gift? Do you say or think, "I give you this gift with the condition that you must keep it forever regardless of how much you like or dislike it, or how it fits your life?" We've yet to hear anyone say that's what they do. So our next question is – Do you think the same is true for gifts you've received? Gifts are typically given with the intention of bringing pleasure and expressing love and thoughtfulness, not with conditions or expectations that they be kept forever.

When you part with a gift, bless the person who gave it to you, bless the intention with which it was given, and bless the new recipient who will experience much joy having it in his/her life. You might even consider doing it in writing in your gratitude journal.

DEALING WITH SPACE PARTNERS

Knowing that we are energetically affected by our stuff, it stands to reason that we are also energetically affected by stuff that doesn't even belong to us. Choosing and creating Conscious Simplicity for our self is one thing, but unless we live alone, most likely we will also be dealing with the challenge of other people's stuff. Dealing with space partners (anyone we share space with) who are not on board can be challenging, but the tips below can help you along the way.

Remember the only person you can change is yourself. No amount of preaching, nagging, begging, demanding or threatening will create lasting change in an unwilling space partner (or anyone else for that matter), but there is good news. While you can't force change on someone who doesn't want it or see the need for it, when you take full responsibility for making the changes you want to make in your own life, you create energy shifts that can't help but affect those around you. But remember you simply cannot dictate when and how it will happen. This is another opportunity to drink from the cup of forgiveness and to practice acceptance.

Clearly define what you want for yourself and from your partner(s). Once you have made the decision to move toward

Conscious Simplicity and have taken the time to clearly define what you want for yourself, you also need to spend some time to get clear about what you want from your space partner(s). The more specific you can be, the better. For instance, maybe you know that you want your partner to help de-clutter your shared bedroom closet, but what is it you specifically want or need from him or her? Do you want your partner to go through their old clothes and donate what they no longer use? Do you want them to move their sports equipment to the basement or to box up their old books? Getting as specific as you possibly can before you approach your partner will be a good start.

Communicate and negotiate. Once you are clear about what you want, it's your responsibility to communicate that to your partner(s). Unless you live with a mind reader, you cannot assume they know what you want or why you want it. Communicate your wants and needs as clearly as you possibly can. Be willing to share your intention. It may not influence your partner in the way you wish, but you will have communicated why it's important to you and your values. Then be willing to negotiate. Be willing to listen to their perspective. Look for ways that you can both (or all) win. Remember, it's also about relationship, which hopefully carries an over-arching intention. If your partner can't seem to part with the pile of old record albums taking up much needed space in your living room, see if you can negotiate a win-win solution. Maybe he/she would be willing to keep only their favorites, or to find a spot to store them in a less communal space.

Set Boundaries. Know your limits and be willing to set your boundaries. If for example, your children resist clearing their own clutter and you have no desire to continually argue about it, set your boundaries about where they may keep their stuff. If they are steadfastly resistant to part with the things that are bothering you, they may have to confine those things to their own bedroom. Or, you may have to set limits on allowing new stuff to come in to your home until they have made room for it by releasing some of the old stuff.

Consistently model the desired behavior. If you want your space partner(s) on board with Conscious Simplicity, seeing you release your unwanted stuff, letting go of your own clutter, and staying conscious of what you bring into your space will affect them more than you know. As you model Conscious Simplicity in your own life, those around you will begin to notice the positive changes taking place and they will feel the shift in your energy. When this happens they may very well want to begin to make changes in their own behaviors.

Make a conscious choice to stay grounded in your own energy. It can be easy to get caught up in trying to get your space partner(s) on board with what you want. Whether or not that happens, commit to staying firmly grounded in your own energy, and remember how it is you want to feel in your space. Do your best to stay in that feeling and create an environment that will support your desire. If peace and calm are what you are want, the more peaceful and calm you can stay, no matter what is going on around you, the more likely it is that your physical space will also eventually begin to reflect those feelings. The chances of you creating a peaceful space from an angry or chaotic mindset are virtually none, so it's important to get your own energy in alignment with the energy of what you want to create.

What to Do with the Stuff

The list of possibilities for finding homes for the things you are releasing is endless and any attempts to name them all would result in certain omissions. So let us offer some general ideas to help you think about options for getting rid of your stuff.

There are wonderful non-profit organizations who take our unwanted stuff and re-sell or give it to others. These non-profits exist in every community where dedicated individuals work tirelessly to fill a desperate need. Many are well known, while others are not so apparent. They can be churches, schools, organizations, libraries, animal shelters, homeless shelters, women's shelters, child welfare groups, hospitals, and theater and music groups. If there is a cause important to you, check online or within your community to see if there are any donation centers committed to that cause. Knowing who will benefit from your donated items can help make releasing them easier and very gratifying.

Consignment shops are another avenue for recycling things – whether it be clothes, furniture, or household goods – and that might provide you a little money in the process. Consignment stores require that items be in good condition, and typically clothes are accepted for the current season so it's unlikely your winter coats will be taken for consignment in May or June.

A garage sale can be a source of income also, but it should be considered carefully. It's not unusual for individuals to place a much higher value on their stuff than what the public is willing to pay, particularly at garage sales, and you may not realize the sums you expect from a sale. The time required to set up and conduct a sale and then dispose of items not purchased can often be quite time consuming. Do the math to determine if the time invested versus the money earned is worth your effort. If none of that matters and you enjoy coordinating a garage sale, by all means go for it!

The popularity of online sales affords another opportunity for disposing of items. Ebay, Craigslist, and Etsy are three that come readily to mind. Amazon Marketplace allows sellers to market their items on the Amazon website also. Posting items on Facebook has become more and more popular as people reach out to friends to buy and sell or simply give away items. Freecycle.com is another great avenue for giving away unwanted items. For online sales you want to consider the investment of time to prepare, list, and ship the item, as well as any security risks with individuals coming to your home.

Many items that aren't appropriate for donation, sale or consignment can be recycled. Check local resources for electronic, paper, and hazardous material recycling. Often county waste management centers offer recycling services. Keep your eyes open for community recycling and shredding events.

The point here is that releasing your stuff doesn't necessarily mean it just gets thrown out. There is so much need in the world and knowing that you can help fill that need is rewarding. It doesn't matter if it's through a unique charity or a well-known donation organization. They are all here to help those who need the stuff that we don't. So resist overthinking about where to take your unwanted items and letting it become an excuse for holding onto them.

CHAPTER 7

WHAT TO EXPECT WHEN YOU RELEASE THE CLUTTER

"Times of transition are strenuous, but I love them. They are an opportunity to purge, rethink priorities, and be intentional about new habits. We can make our new normal any way we want."

~KRISTIN ARMSTRONG

IT WOULD BE wonderful if we could say that when you let go of your stuff, you'll feel absolutely great and will find yourself doing a happy dance. While that may be true to some degree, it's not necessarily the total story. Many unexpected emotions, feelings, and physical reactions can surface as you go through the process of releasing. If you know what to expect, you won't be surprised or disappointed about what comes up.

Because we are energetically connected to the things around us, we can expect a shift in our energy when we release our stuff. With those shifts, we may even experience physical symptoms. And because there is a connection between physical clutter and mental and emotional clutter, it's not unusual that releasing our stuff triggers many emotional symptoms too, some more pleasant than others. Being aware of what's happening, however, can make dealing with the reactions much easier.

Dallas had no idea the changes that lie ahead when she made that first conscious choice to begin releasing what no longer served her. While her story may seem extreme, it's a good example of some of the temporary physical and emotional symptoms we can experience as we clear the clutter from our home and from our life.

Dallas came to the women's group gathering quite confident that she didn't have much clutter in her life. Her home was neat and clean; she didn't enjoy shopping, wasn't into acquiring a lot of unnecessary things, and didn't feel much emotional attachment to her possessions. She didn't expect to personally gain a lot from the class, but was happy to be there as a support to the other women in the group. She sat quietly throughout most of the evening, even as the other women shared their stories and "aha" moments, but it was clear there was something going on inside her head, something she didn't immediately share with the group. She went home that evening with a new perspective on clutter and, as she describes it, compelled to go through each room in her home, one at a time, and to purge anything that she no longer used or loved.

That purging began the very next day. Dallas chose her home office as her starting point and immediately jumped in, finding many surprises along the way. Boxes of paperwork and tax returns from a business she and her husband no longer owned and for which the IRS requirement had long since passed; a checkbook, checks and check register from a bank account she had closed fifteen years prior; and plaques, service awards, and an old name plate from a job she was very happy to have left more than twenty years before. These were just some of the things she discovered tucked neatly away in file cabinets, boxes or closets in that office, none of which she had any desire to keep.

During the next couple of days, as Dallas continued her clearing, she began feeling both physically and mentally exhausted, quite overwhelmed and even physically dizzy. When she reached out to us, we encouraged her to practice self-care, to pace herself and to pay attention to what was coming up for her.

One of the things that came up for Dallas in the process of cleaning out that office was the memory of how overwhelmed and stressed she was during the entire seven years that she kept the books, filed the quarterly taxes and coordinated the scheduling for her husband's construction business, all the while working another demanding job at a nearby university. It was during that time that she first began experiencing chronic shoulder and neck pain, as well as chronic fatigue, and she was even able to pinpoint the exact day her symptoms began. It was the first day she set up the business.

As Dallas continued clearing out the old paperwork, more memories of that stressful time began to surface, resulting in an increased intensity of her chronic neck and shoulder pain. There was a connection she could not deny between that stressful time and her failing health that made her even more determined to release anything and everything connected to the business. She enlisted some help with the heavy lifting, removed everything that was moveable from that space, including bookcases and file cabinets that were no longer necessary. She added back only the things she really wanted to keep, recycled what she could, and burned the rest in her backyard burn pit. But Dallas had only just begun.

Once the clearing was complete, Dallas was able to see that old office space with new eyes and she was struck with a new vision for it. She painted, redecorated, performed an energy shifting ritual and created something in that space she had always wanted for herself, a meditation and writing room. This room that once represented an extremely stressful time in her past was transformed into a place of peace, relaxation and healing. A place Dallas could go to rejuvenate and nurture her soul. Talk about a shift in energy!

As those changes occurred, Dallas also became aware of other changes she had been putting off in her life. Within a few months she found a way *to leave the job she had long ago outgrown but never believed she could let go. While money was tight for a while, the income she lost when she left her job was soon replaced in unexpected ways. In less than a year since she began, every room in Dallas's home was cleared and transformed, and so was her life. As she consciously cleared each room, new visions were born until one by one each room in her home felt peaceful and beautiful to her. Most of the changes she made were inexpensive as she enlisted the help of friends, learned new DIY skills, and put her thrift shopping abilities to good use, but there were even a few, long overdue renovations that she was able to have done along the way.*

Dallas learned a lot about herself as she moved through the process of consciously simplifying and experienced a great deal of emotional and physical healing along the way. Her health continued to improve, she was able to tap into her spiritual and creative sides for the first time in years and there has been a definitive shift in her energy visible to anyone who knows her. Dallas' story may be one of the most extreme we witnessed, both in terms of the physical and emotional symptoms experienced and the personal change, but we do not doubt the connection between the physical transformation of her home and the energetic transformation of her life.

EMOTIONAL SYMPTOMS

FEAR AND ANXIETY

The fear we talked about in Chapter Three that keeps the clutter energy stuck can surface again as we let that clutter energy go. The process of releasing our stuff can trigger the fear of not having enough now or at some future point in time, or the fear of making a mistake and discarding something important. We fear not knowing who we are without the stuff we identify with. We fear letting go of our past and we even fear hurting someone's feelings if we let go of something they have given us. We may also fear the vulnerability we face when our clutter no longer shields us from the world outside of us. The further we take the fear-based reactions, the more likely it is that we will also experience fear's big, ugly co-conspirator – anxiety, as we dwell on our decisions and try to second guess whether they were right or not. We can easily create a flurry of churning anxiety for ourselves by holding tightly to our fears.

ANGER

It can be surprising when anger pops up in the process of releasing our stuff. Again, this is most likely because of the memories associated with the thing we are trying to release. If you find anger creeping in, it can be helpful to ask yourself if you have been hanging onto any anger toward someone or something from the past. Are you angry about a dream that never came true, or a relationship that ended? Are you angry at yourself for all the money you spent on clothes never worn or that no longer fit, or tools you've never used, or the stuff you bought to make yourself feel better? Are you angry that you have worked hard, at a job you don't enjoy for too many years and feel you don't have much to show for it? Be willing to notice where the anger is coming from, and how forgiveness can play a role in releasing that anger (see Chapter Five).

NOSTALGIA

There is nothing wrong with being sentimental, but when our sometimes-idealized memories of the past keep us from letting go and moving into our future, our nostalgia is not serving us well. Chances are you are not really as attached to the ticket stubs from the first concert you ever attended as you are to the feeling you associate with that experience. What emotion does this evoke that you are wishing to feel again? Maybe it's the excitement that you felt that night. Maybe it's the sense of freedom that came with dancing to the music in the open air so long ago. Maybe it's the feeling of connectedness you shared with the others in the audience. And maybe, just maybe, what you are feeling nostalgic about is a simpler, more carefree time in your life.

Your nostalgia has an important message for you. It's telling you that there is something you want to feel again, or at least feel more of. This is not about the ticket stubs! It's about the feelings they bring up for you. The question then becomes, how can I bring more excitement or freedom, or connectedness, or simplicity into my present life. Try to stay open to the message that is coming through for you. It can contribute to setting clear intentions.

Guilt

Often we feel guilty and ungrateful when we discard things, especially if it was a gift, or we spent a considerable amount of money for it, or we just don't like it anymore. Remember, it's perfectly possible to be grateful for the enjoyment we once experienced from something as we are consciously releasing that very thing. It's absolutely possible to acknowledge the purpose our stuff once held for us at the same time we let it go. Releasing something does not negate that purpose or our gratitude for it. Letting go with gratitude is simply a statement to the Universe that we are moving forward, expanding and evolving, just as we are meant to do in life.

Sadness/Depression

Sadness or depression may also creep in when the memories we associate with the stuff arise. This is often the case when we release

the things of past relationships. Whether it was a romantic connection that faded or a family member who passed, we can experience a heaviness in our hearts when we let go. Know that you can
honor the memories and keep them in your heart without hanging
onto the stuff.

EXCITEMENT/ANTICIPATION
There is often a sense of excitement and/or anticipation that comes
with the process of letting go of the stuff we've been hanging on
to for too long. Whenever we release something, we are making
room for something even better to come into our life and that is
exciting, even when we have no idea what might be coming to us
next. And then there is the excitement that can come from just
having created more space in our life.

RELIEF
When we finally let something go, it's not unusual to feel a big
sense of relief. That's because as we release our stuff, we are also
releasing the energy attached to it. Whether or not we have even
been aware of how that old energy has been affecting us, we will
most likely feel the difference once it's gone. We are also likely to
feel relief for the additional physical and emotional space we have
created for our self.

FREEDOM
The sense of freedom that can come from not having to think or
deal with the stuff anymore when we release it can take us by surprise. Often we're not even aware of the energetic burden we've
been carrying until it is gone and we taste the sweetness of the
simplicity we are creating in our life.

PHYSICAL SYMPTOMS

As Dallas' story showed, sometimes the shift in energy that occurs when we release our stuff can temporarily bring on physical symptoms too, once again some more pleasant than others. If you find yourself experiencing fatigue, headaches, muscle aches and/ or light-headedness during the releasing process, it is most likely that your body is just adjusting to the energetic shift that is happening for you. Your body may even feel as if it's in a tug of war between the old and new energy. And it could be you're just tired from all the work you've done! This will pass once your body has time to adjust and then you may very well find yourself experiencing a renewed sense of calming energy, empowerment and clear headedness.

SELF-CARE

"You cannot pour from an empty cup."

~UNKNOWN

There may be times throughout the process of embracing Conscious Simplicity that life actually feels more complicated and more cluttered, and anything but simple. We often refer to it as the "chaos before the calm." Not only is it because we're moving our stuff around, but because anytime we make changes, anytime we shift the energy of our life, things tend to get messy for a bit. Don't let this throw you because it is temporary. One of the things we know from working with clients as they go about the releasing process is just how important self-care is, both during and after the process. Below are some self-care tools that we have shared with clients and have found to be helpful.

- Ground yourself with some deep breathing
- Enlist the support of a trusted friend, even if that just means checking in by phone
- Forgive yourself for past mistakes (wasted time, money or energy)
- Keep your sense of humor
- Check in with yourself often and acknowledge when you need a break
- Get enough rest
- Eat healthy
- Drink lots of water
- Get outside and breathe some fresh air
- Reward yourself. Celebrate what you have accomplished each step of the way.
- Put on some music, sing, dance or listen to a favorite radio show as you go. Make it fun!
- Let it go. Once it's done, don't look back. Don't second-guess yourself!
- Allow for a period of adjustment as the energy shifts.

The bottom line is take care of yourself whether you're releasing inner or outer clutter. Self-care is a necessity.

CHAPTER 8

RELEASING NON-PHYSICAL CLUTTER

"Clutter isn't just the stuff in your closet. It's anything that gets between you and the life that you want to be living."

~ PETER WALSH

SINCE OUR NON-PHYSICAL clutter is typically intangible, it can be more difficult to recognize, yet it can be just as overwhelming and keep us just as stuck as physical clutter does. Therefore, we might have to be willing to delve into some uncomfortable places in order to bring our inner clutter into our awareness. Self-awareness does not have to be painful, but it does require honesty and taking the time to look at what is going on.

EXPLORING YOUR INVISIBLE CLUTTER

We touched on different types of non-physical clutter in Chapter Two, but before we look at the preparation and process of releasing that non-physical clutter, let's take a deeper look, through a series of questions, at some of the ways it may be showing up in our life.

Negative or limiting beliefs: Beliefs are just thoughts we continue to think until they become our truth. Are you aware of the beliefs or self-talk that are holding you back? Which of these are you willing to challenge? If you had to choose just one of your beliefs to change, which one would it be? What new thought, belief, or self-talk would you choose to replace it with. How might changing that belief help simplify your life?

Grudges: Is there anyone or anything in your life you have not been willing to forgive? Are you holding onto any grudges or resentments? Have you been withholding forgiveness from yourself in anyway? What have you been telling yourself must happen before you can offer forgiveness to yourself or another? How might simply choosing to let go of a grudge or resentment or offer unconditional forgiveness simplify your life?

Guilt: Have you been holding onto guilt about anything? Is there anything you can do now to correct the situation that is the source of that guilt? If so, are you willing to take the necessary steps to correct it? What purpose is the guilt serving in your life? Is hanging onto the guilt making things better for you or anyone else? What would you gain by releasing the guilt? What steps would you need to take in order to let it go?

Being controlling: How much of your time and energy is spent thinking about, talking about, worrying about and trying to control other people's behavior? How much is spent trying to control the outcome of any situation? Are you able to let go of the outcome of a situation once you've made a reasonable effort to make it work? How might releasing the need to control situations or other people make your life simpler?

Dishonesty and lack of integrity: Are there areas of your life where you are being less than honest? Have you told any big or small untruths that keep coming back to haunt you? Do you sometimes avoid telling the truth to put off dealing with something unpleasant? How much of your time or energy is spent avoiding dealing with something that needs to be addressed? Do you keep your word? How is your life simpler when your actions are in alignment with what you believe to be right?

Enabling others: There is a critical difference between being supportive and being an enabler. Being supportive does not drain your energy or make you feel responsible for someone else's well-being. Are you able to let others take responsibility for their own behavior and their own life? How much of your own time and energy is spent trying to right the wrongs of someone you care about, or trying to save them from themselves? How often are you the one left cleaning up the life messes of others, rather than letting them experience the natural consequences of their actions? In what ways might you be caught in the trap of enabling another? How much simpler would your life be if you released the need to save others from themselves? What else could you do with the time and energy you spend enabling another?

The need for approval: How much of your time and energy is spent wondering or worrying about what others think of you? Are you driven by a need to have others like you? Is there anyone in particular you have been trying too hard to please? Do you sometimes fail to speak your truth for fear of being perceived negatively by others? How might your life be simplified by releasing some or all of your need for approval?

Out of balance relationships: Are you mindful of the company you keep? Are you mostly spending time with people you enjoy or is your time taken up by people you don't even care to be around? Which of your friendships/relationships feel authentic to you? Have you outgrown some friendships, but have not left them behind? How might releasing outgrown, unhealthy or unbalanced friendships/relationships simplify your life?

Chronic complaining: Do you spend your time and energy complaining about things you have no control over? Do you talk through and process situations that bother or upset you with someone you trust in order to gain a better understanding and move on, or do you continue to complain about the same things over and over again with no intention of making any changes? Do you find that you bond with others over mutual complaining about your boss, the opposite sex, your spouse, the government/politicians, the state of the world in general, or anything else? What would you have room for in your life if you released the chronic complaining?

Assuming, rather than asking: How often do you take offense to something someone said or did because you assume their words or actions were intended to offend you? Do you take the time to clarify when you are not completely clear about someone's expectations or intentions, either at work or in your personal life, or do you proceed without the clarity you need? How might it simplify your life to ask, rather than assume, when you are not completely clear about something?

Overthinking and second guessing decisions: Do you often complicate your decision making process by overthinking every detail and trying to anticipate every possible way something could go wrong? Do you often fear making the wrong decision? Do you run around asking everyone else's opinion about what you should do? Once you've made a decision, do you waste your precious time and energy second guessing it? It's one thing to be mindful and informed with your decisions and quite another to torture yourself through the process. How might you simplify your decision making process? Can you imagine just trusting that you will make the best of whatever decision you make, and then simply allow yourself to let it go and be at peace? How might this simplify your life?

Word Clutter: How often do you use more words than necessary? Are you just talking, or actually communicating? Do you sometimes talk just to fill a void when you actually have nothing to say? Do you ever talk, or continue to talk, well beyond what is necessary in order to gain attention or to keep the focus on yourself? Do you sometimes over explain yourself? How might it simplify your life to release the word clutter?

Noise Clutter: Do you mindlessly leave the TV or radio on in order to avoid being alone with your own thoughts? Have you become immune to the unnecessary noise going on all around you, or are you making conscious choices about what you are willing to listen to? What might you gain from experiencing a little silence everyday?

Gossip clutter: How much of your precious time and energy do you spend participating in gossip, either by simply listening to it, or by sharing it with others? Do you use gossip as a way of bonding with others? What need is the gossip clutter filling in your life? Is there a way that you could use that time and energy that would serve you better?

E-clutter: Is your inbox overflowing with old emails? Is your day constantly interrupted because you have your phone set on instant alert for text message, emails, social media posts, and breaking news? When was the last time you cleaned up your computer files, deleted old phone numbers and voicemail messages, took a few minute to block incoming spam or tried turning off your instant alerts? How might clearing some of the e-clutter simplify your life?

Information clutter: How much news are you watching or listening to in a day? Do you find yourself watching the same footage of natural disasters, terrorist attacks and other horrors over and over again, just because the news stations continue to play them? Are you staying mindful that advertising is designed to convince you that you are inadequate (too old, too fat, too skinny, dull hair, potential body odor, or not-so-white teeth) without their particular product? Are you allowing yourself to be inundated with ads from pharmaceutical companies that purposefully trigger worry about every disease or ailment you could possibly end up with in this lifetime? How much of your energy and peace of mind do you give away to media information on a daily basis? How might clearing some of the information clutter simplify your life?

Time clutter: Are you staying mindful of how you spend your time? Is it in alignment with the things you value most? Are you spending a significant amount of your time on activities and self-imposed obligations you don't really care about? How much of your time do you give away begrudgingly, rather than just saying "no"? What would be the first piece of time clutter you would like to release? How would you use the time created by releasing it? How might that simplify your life?

Focusing on the past: How much of your time and energy are you putting into focusing on the past? What old story do you repeatedly tell as if it were a recent event? How much of your identity, your worth, or your attention do you place on a previous time in your life? How much time do you spend longing for the way things used to be? What would it be like to release the tight grip on the past and create room for the present? How might that simplify your life?

Worrying about the future: How many of your present moments are being cluttered up with worry about the future? Do you routinely identify the potential worst-case scenario in any given situation? Do you believe that you can stop bad things from happening by obsessively worrying about them? Are you confused about the difference between planning for the future and worrying about the future? Do you clutter up today by worrying about tomorrow? How might releasing the worry habit simplify your life?

Self-denial: Do you ever complicate your life by denying yourself something you really need or that would make your life simpler? Do you deny yourself things that bring you joy, even when you can afford them? How often do you put off replacing or repairing items that make your day-to-day life easier? How often does that end up costing you more in time, energy and money in the long run? Have you ever put off a car repair so long that you ended up stranded at the most inconvenient time? How might releasing the self-denial help simplify your life?

Multi-tasking: Have you fallen into the trap of multi-tasking in order to get more done in the course of a day? Are you scattering your energy in several directions at once, rather than focusing on one thing at a time? Do you pride yourself in being able to do several things at once, even though it has actually been proven to be counterproductive? How might letting go of multi-tasking, and instead focusing on one thing at a time help simplify your life?

Body clutter: Are you staying mindful of how your body feels after ingesting certain foods or other indulgences, or ignoring the signs it so wisely gives you? Are you paying attention when your body is hungry or thirsty and when it is satisfied? Do you jump on the bandwagon with every new diet or food program that comes along, rather than learning to listen to and trust your body? Are most of your meals consumed on the run, or do you take the time to enjoy them? Do you recognize what makes your body feel drained, what makes it feel energized, and when it needs to rest? Do you honor your body's need for sleep, as well as it's need for movement? Have you taken the time to notice what type of movement your body enjoys most (dancing, walking, swimming, yoga, kick boxing, etc.) or do you engage in every new exercise trend, even if you don't enjoy it? Do you avoid exercise all together? Do you honor the wisdom of your body and the goldmine of information it holds for you? How might your life be simplified by releasing the body clutter?

Financial clutter: Do you conduct yourself with financial integrity by making conscious choices about your spending, or do you often make ill-conceived purchases? Do you pay your bills on time whenever possible, or do you make a habit of racking up late fees? Do you make an honest effort to live within your means, or do you pile up debt? When was the last time you took a good look at your budget or areas where you could reduce unnecessary spending? How might life be simpler if you chose to clean up your financial clutter?

Drama clutter: Do you find yourself getting upset often, either by your own drama or that of others? Are there certain people in your life who expect you to listen to or participate in their latest perceived crisis on a regular basis? Do you expect others to listen to or participate in your latest perceived crisis on a regular basis? Do you find yourself jumping into the middle of other people's problems, rather than tending to your own life? How might your life be simpler if you let go of the drama clutter?

Spiritual clutter: Have you taken the time to determine what really nourishes your spirit or are you just going through the motions spiritually? Have you found a spiritual practice that fully nourishes your soul or are you trying to live up to someone else's expectations by spending time following traditions that don't resonate with you? How might your life be simplified by identifying which of your spiritual beliefs and practices feel authentic to you and which do not?

There are certainly other ways to complicate our life with invisible clutter, but these are the most common. If more come to mind for you, you may want to take a moment to note them. You may also even want to simply ask yourself, "In what other ways am I unnecessarily complicating my life?" And then trust what comes up for you.

While each piece of non-physical clutter is, in itself, important to recognize, it can be especially enlightening to see the entire picture of our invisible clutter. With that in mind we've created a tool, My Invisible Clutter Inventory, in the Resources section to help you summarize your intangible clutter and the benefits of releasing each piece.

The Preparation

Releasing our non-physical clutter can require opening our minds and our hearts like never before and it sometimes takes a leap of faith, but being prepared can be very helpful. Let's take a look at some helpful ways to prepare for the process of letting that non-physical clutter go.

Slow down and get quiet. Staying overly busy is actually one of the ways we avoid self-awareness. We can't be expected to explore the things we find uncomfortable to look at when our schedules are filled to the brim, now can we? Commit to creating the time and the silence for some self-exploration. Find a quiet place where you won't be distracted or interrupted, get comfortable, shake off the craziness of the day, and simply breathe for a bit.

Be willing to get real with yourself. Examining our grudges, relationships, negative attitudes, outdated beliefs, and mindless habits require getting brutally honest with our self and taking full responsibility for our own life. Getting real with our self can be uncomfortable, but it helps to remember that this is about self-awareness, not perfection. It also helps to keep in mind that the payoffs are well worth any discomfort we may experience as we move toward our most authentic life.

Be willing to challenge your old stories. Just as with the release of physical clutter, our emotional clutter requires letting go of old stories. We all have stories about our own personal limitations, stories about what we believe we deserve or don't deserve, stories about what we believe we can or can't have and stories about what we believe is or isn't possible for us. All of which can keep us stuck. When we recognize those old stories for what they are and are willing to challenge them, we have room to create new and better stories for our self that help us move forward.

I (Teresa) have told myself many stories in my life, and I can tell you that they all felt true for me at the time. But when I made the conscious decision to challenge and release the old stories that were not serving me well, I created the space in my life for new stories that did. One of the stories I told myself for years after my divorce was that I had acted selfishly by not waiting until my sons were grown to leave my marriage. That story translated into me carrying around a lot of guilt and the belief that I should never put myself first in any circumstance again because putting myself first would cause pain to others. That old story was triggered again for me when I was deciding to give away the glassware that had been a Mother's Day gift from my sons so many years before, and that I wrote about in the introduction of this book. But when I chose to question the validity of that old story, to let it go and to tell myself a new story that served me better, I was also able to release emotional clutter that went along with it.

So what new story did I tell myself? My new story is that putting myself first is mandatory because it is what allows me to thrive, and when I thrive I am in a much better position to be there for others when they need me. When I put myself first I become a better mom, a better wife, a better friend and a better person.

In order to let go of the guilt and other baggage I had attached to that Mother's Day gift and carried for so many years, I also needed to rewrite the story I had been telling myself about my connection with my sons. Somehow I had convinced myself that our connection could be broken by the physical distance between us. What I now know is this. The connection I have with my sons cannot be broken, no matter where life takes any of us, and it certainly is not dependent upon me keeping a particular Mother's Day gift for the rest of my life!

That was just one of the stories I had told myself over the years and it was just one of the ways I was cluttering up my life and staying stuck. Releasing that old story required slowing down, getting real with myself about some emotional baggage I had been carrying, and challenging some of the things I had told myself for a long time. Can you identify an old story you have been telling yourself? What new story could you replace it with?

Assess your willingness to make changes. While we often think it's hard to let go of our physical stuff, we can be just as resistant to let go of our inner clutter too. The need to make changes in relationships, release old habits, and/or say "no" to unrealistic expectations or demands on our time, whether they are coming from our self or others, are just a few of the discoveries we might make in the process of examining our non-physical clutter. As empowering as it can be to consciously choose to make changes in our life, it can also be quite unsettling at times. If we are not ready for the change and willing to do what it takes to make that change happen, self-sabotage is likely. As we talked about in Chapter Four, we can assess the gap between our readiness and willingness with these simple questions: "On a scale of 1 to 10 how ready am I? And on that same scale how willing am I to do what is necessary?"

Begin thinking quality over quantity. As with our physical possessions, it's also helpful to think quality over quantity when it comes to how we spend our time and energy. For example, being willing to take a look at which of our friendships/relationships are based on a foundation of trust, respect, compatibility and other values we cherish, and which of our activities are meaningful and satisfying to us, will help focus our perspective on quality rather than quantity. That awareness helps us make choices about what we want to keep and what we want to release.

Breakdown the benefits of letting it go. As we begin to identify the non-physical clutter in our life, take a moment to consider and acknowledge what we might gain with each piece we choose to release. For example, what might we gain by releasing the habit of mindless spending? More financial freedom? The ability to save extra cash toward that vacation we've been wanting to take? What will we gain from releasing the belief that we must say "yes" to every request for our time? Is it perhaps some much-needed downtime and more opportunity to relax? Maybe it's more peace of mind or simply more energy for activities we actually do enjoy. Identifying what we will gain with each release will help us get to that critical "why" as we set our intention.

Set the intention and goal(s). Just as with the preparation for releasing physical clutter, preparing to release our non-physical clutter requires clarity about our intention and goal(s). Remember, setting our intention forces us to identify why it is important to make the changes we are choosing to make and setting our goals will support us in that intention.

The Process

Our process for letting go of the invisible clutter in our life will most likely look unlike anyone else's. There is no single right way to go about releasing our non-physical clutter, but keeping the following tips in mind as we find our way through our own unique process will be helpful.

Choose your starting point. Once again, it can be helpful to start small. Cleaning out your old emails might be an easier place to start than cleaning out your unhealthy relationships. Releasing unnecessary activities might be an easier starting point than releasing your grudges. Your starting point is up to you. Trust your inner guidance on this.

Forget about doing it right. This is your process and you get to choose how to go about it. Again, trust yourself. Honor yourself. Be flexible with yourself.

Stay mindful of your intention. Remember that staying conscious of your intention, your "why" as you work toward each goal can make the critical difference in whether or not you reach that goal. Keep your eye on the prize.

Stay in the moment. Releasing your non-physical clutter is about being in the present, not looking backward or forward. Keep in mind that any energy you put into dwelling on what has happened in the past or worry about what could happen in the future will take away from the energy you could be putting into creating the life you want now.

Be kind to yourself along the way. This could be a messy process. Beating yourself up when you find yourself slipping back into old habits or belief systems will not be helpful. Lovingly recognizing when you are doing so, then consciously choosing to treat yourself with compassion is the only way to get unstuck.

Ask for the help you need. Some things are harder to let go of than others, especially things we've been clinging to for a lifetime. It can be difficult to let go of our emotional stuff, old habits or unhealthy relationships. It helps to be patient and kind to our self, but sometimes we need to reach out for support too. Support can come from a trusted friend or loved one, or a professional. Sometimes just having someone hear our story can help us let it go. Give yourself permission to ask for the help you need and to tell your story, just don't get stuck in it. Here's a good rule of thumb. If you've told your story so many times that even you are starting to find it boring, it's time to let it go and move on. If you can't do that on your own, get the help you need.

CHAPTER 9

SACRED SPACES

"Your sacred space is where you can find yourself again and again.

~ JOSEPH CAMPBELL"

ALL SPACE IS SACRED

As WE EMBRACE Conscious Simplicity and consider clearing out our physical spaces, it's important to remember that all space is sacred, if we recognize it and treat it so. That realization became very clear to Teresa when she was fortunate enough to take a long anticipated trip to the beautiful island of Kauai with two of her good friends.

One of the adventures we all looked forward to was a guided tour of "the most sacred places on the island." We all expected that something incredibly magical would happen and that we would be awestruck with the sacredness of the sights we were to see and learn about. While the beauty of those sights was absolutely breathtaking, and learning about their history was fascinating, I came away with a new perspective about what really makes a space sacred.

As I listened to the tour guide describe the sacredness of each location, I did feel some amazing energy, but I also was struck with a deep sadness that we were declaring any space to be more sacred than another. That night in our shared hotel room, my friend, Joanne, and I talked about the beauty and sacredness of our own home state. We realized that we had been taking for granted something that was very sacred to our hearts - home. We had been so focused on escaping the frigid February temperatures and piles of snow we left behind in Michigan that we lost sight of what we loved about our home state. The amazing beaches; the rich history of the Great Lakes; the nurturing spirit of the Midwest; the gorgeous, hot summer days; the unbelievable rebirth of nature that occurs each spring just when we're sure we will never see a live flower again; and the unbelievable colors and fresh breezes of autumn. We even came to realize that the frigid winter weather serves us well by slowing us down, especially the snow filled days that sometimes force us to stay home against our will.

We were both homesick at the moment. Not because we didn't love Kauai in all its beauty, and not because we didn't recognize what was sacred about the island. But because we also realized that our homes were sacred too, and we both were struck with the knowing that we never wanted to take that for granted again. I have traveled a bit since that trip to Kauai, and I always enjoy experiencing new places, but what I will never do again is forget that no space is more sacred than another or just how sacred home is to me. Even in the dead cold of a Michigan winter!

OUR OWN PERSONAL SACRED SPACE

We all deserve and need our own sacred space. We all deserve and need a place that is safe and beautiful and that feeds our soul. Whether we live in a house, a condo, an apartment, a mobile home or lakeside palace, it can and should be our sacred soft place to land in a world that is not always so soft.

When we see our home as sacred space and treat it as such by staying conscious of what we bring into it, it will serve us well. It will not burden us. It will help to center us, ground us and reconnect us with who we really are so that we are better equipped to take our unique gifts into the world on a daily basis. Home is not just where we drop our stuff. It is our sanctuary from the outside world. No matter where we live, what we can or can't afford, or with whom we share our space, we have the opportunity to create our own sacred, soft place to land. When we keep our home clear of physical and non-physical clutter, we are honoring and respecting it as the sacred space it is meant to be. When we embrace Conscious Simplicity, we are honoring and respecting who we are and acknowledging that we deserve to experience the sacred in our life.

After my husband died, I (Barbara) was faced with living alone for the first time in my life. After graduating from high school, I lived in a college dorm with a roommate. I married immediately after leaving college, and when that marriage ended in divorce, I lived with my young son. We were alone together eleven years before we became family with my second husband. Four years later my son was off to college and Gerry and I moved to Florida the following year. It wasn't until seven years after Gerry and I made the move to Florida that I faced a significant first of living alone. It was, at times, a daunting and uncomfortable thought.

I remember how unsettled I was during those months after Gerry's death. Certainly the grief from my loss played into the unrest but I also felt out of place. Our home had been our place and there was no more "our." I was trying to figure out how I fit into our space by myself, how I fit into the world of couple relationships we had formed, and how I fit into the routines we had established together. Because I made the decision to move back to Indianapolis shortly after he died, I didn't spend time much defining my sacred space in Florida. As you recall from Chapter Four, I had laser-focus on selling the house and making a cross-country move! But on some level I knew that my new home would be a place that would wrap me in peacefulness, serenity, and comfort and at the same time open itself to the love and friendship of family and friends who would come to visit. My intention was to create a space and a life where being alone did not mean I was lonely. I created that space and that life and experience a wonderful contentment living alone, while being in close proximity to family and friends and enjoying their companionship when they visit. I constantly reevaluate what brings me joy and comfort in my home and I am in an ongoing process of releasing what doesn't support that joy and bringing in that which does. I've come to value my alone time as a time to renew my energies, refocus my direction and reaffirm my gratitude for all that I have. And I appreciate the fact that because I often work from home, I have sacred space to support me in that endeavor. To me my home is a sacred place of warmth and comfort and I never tire of being there.

HEALING SPACE AS SACRED SPACE

The topic of "healing spaces" is especially near and dear to my heart because I (Teresa) have experienced first-hand the benefit of a sacred healing space when I recovered from knee replacement surgery. Having put this surgery off much longer than I ever should have since the original injury occurred when I was a child, I finally made peace with the idea of having it done. But I was taken back a bit when my surgeon was able to schedule it just one week out from my first office visit. Yikes! Since I had every intention of experiencing a quick, peaceful and full recovery, I had some preparing to do!

Knowing that other than a night or two in the hospital, my recovery would be happening at home, and knowing how strongly I am affected by my surroundings, a well-intentioned healing space was crucial. In the week leading up to my surgery, I prepared a space in my home, making sure that it was not only extra clean and clutter free, but comfortable, peaceful and held some beautiful things for me to enjoy. I also indulged in some special sheets, pajamas, loungewear and slippers in order to make the healing process as enjoyable as possible. Even though I would have limited mobility, I consciously chose an area of my home that didn't have a television in it to spend the bulk of my days. I made this choice because I didn't want to fall into the trap of bombarding myself with mindless "noise clutter" as my body healed from the trauma of surgery. Instead of parking myself in front of a television screen all day, I chose a spot with a view of my backyard. Reading and watching the leaves change colors, the squirrels busily gathering nuts for the winter, and an occasional deer munching away at what was left of my fall mums were very peaceful and healing for me. And, while I watched a bit of TV during my recovery period, I was careful to make sure to do so consciously, not just out of habit, boredom, or default.

I knew that if my environment was stressful, my immune system would be burdened and my healing process would be affected. My intention was to create a space that nurtured my mind, my body and my spirit so that I could heal as quickly and completely as possible. Creating my healing space required some introspection and some conscious choices about what is important to me. I was able to identify what I need most in order to heal — quiet, comfort, beauty — and I put some conscious thought into what kinds of things make me feel nurtured. Being surrounded by my favorite colors of red and turquoise, listening to the sounds of nature, and cuddling up in a soft, cozy quilt were a few of the things that I incorporated into my healing space. You might find it healing to be surrounded by beautiful artwork, pictures of loved ones, scented candles, plants, flowers, rocks/stones, flowing water, or other elements of nature. Maybe having access to inspiring books or love stories, listening to certain music, wrapping yourself in a favorite blanket, or hearing the sound of laughter nourishes your soul. Whatever it is that personally makes you feel good will aid in your healing and can consciously be incorporated into your healing space.

The time I spent in the hospital also enhanced my awareness and left me with a much deeper understanding of how important our environment *is to the healing process. My hospital experience was actually quite positive. I had a private room, was well fed and received excellent medical care. No doubt, all of this was important and I was grateful for every bit of it. But, at the same time, I couldn't imagine trying to heal in such a cold and impersonal environment for any significant amount of time. My soul craved the quiet, nurturing space of home and I couldn't help thinking that the world would be a simpler, healthier, kinder, more peaceful place if we all had a healing space of our own. Not just a space to heal from the trauma of surgery, injury or illness, but a space we could retreat to on a regular basis to grieve our losses, lick our wounds, or just recover from the day-to-day stresses of life. A space filled with only the things that nourish our souls and where we could temporarily shut out the noise and distractions of the outside world to heal our emotional, mental and spiritual wounds.*

We invite you to consider creating your own healing space. Of course it would be wonderful if we all had access to our own cozy cottage on the lake or secluded cabin in the woods, but even a quiet corner somewhere in your home could be transformed if you set a conscious intention for the space. To help you identify what your ideal healing space would be like, we've provided a worksheet, Creating a Healing Space, in the Resources section.

Creating our own sacred space and healing space is very much instinctual and there is much to be learned by simply being still and listening to our inner guidance. Our soul already knows what we need in order to live joyfully or to heal. We simply need to allow the wisdom of our soul to flow into our conscious awareness. However, for those interested in learning more about how to bring balance, harmony and positive energy into your living space, we have listed several books on the art of Feng Shui in the Resources section.

DRAMA CLUTTER AND SACRED SPACES

Unnecessary drama can clutter up our life and lower our energy. When we allow the drama clutter into our sacred space, we are not only being disrespectful of our space and our self, we are allowing harmful energy into the very place that is meant to be our sanctuary. Things happen in life, there's no doubt, but when we make a conscious choice not to allow that drama clutter into our home whenever possible, we are taking control of our little corner of the world. Part of embracing Conscious Simplicity means "just saying no" to unnecessary drama. (And, by the way, most drama is unnecessary). In essence, if being around it upsets you, stresses you out, or drains your energy, it can probably be considered drama clutter. Take time to notice how you feel in your space. Ask yourself if you have unknowingly invited drama clutter into your home and let that awareness lead you to make conscious choices about what you are willing to allow in as you move forward. Set your boundaries because nobody else will set them for you.

When I (Teresa) worked as a family social worker and later as a Juvenile Probation Officer, my workdays were filled with more drama than I care to remember. Pretty early into my career, I realized that for my own sake and for the sake of my family, I had to declare my home a drama-free zone. This meant I refused to rehash my workday at home and if I needed to talk about something work related, I would do it elsewhere. I did not allow co-workers to talk shop when they stopped by during non-work hours. I learned to turn off my work cell phone unless I was on call. I stopped watching the nightly news, and would instead pick and choose what news articles I was willing to read. I refused to read any angry or fear based social media posts, and God help any poor soul who attempted to bring any of their own drama into my home. This does not mean I didn't care about what was happening in my friends' lives, but I was, and still am, vigilant about protecting what kind of energy I allow in to my home because my home is sacred to me.

Removing the drama clutter from your home will simplify your life more than you can imagine. Maybe it's not possible to keep all the drama energy out (especially if you have teenagers!), but you can limit it and at the very least you can agree to keep it confined to one room. Making a conscious choice to reduce the unnecessary drama in your sacred space, setting your ground rules, defining your boundaries and sticking to them will go a long way in creating the peaceful energy you deserve to come home to.

WHY BEAUTY IS SACRED

"Remember that any location you are in affects the mind and spirit, therefore your environment is one that should be pleasing to you. Seeing and being a part of a beautiful space makes the mind happy, and a happy state of mind is conducive to delving into your inner discovery."

~ *JAMES VAN PRAAGH*

How we define beauty and what we see as beautiful is very personal. It also changes and evolves as we do but this much is true: beauty is sacred and beauty is necessary if we are to fully live our life. We all need beauty in our life, however we define it for our self. Walks in nature, music that feeds our soul, books that stimulate our imaginations, rooms that soothe our senses, colors that brighten our day, all bring beauty and positive energy into our life. Beauty inspires us, energizes us, and raises our personal vibrations. Surrounding our self with beauty is one of the fastest ways to shift our energy. Think about how we naturally gravitate to beautiful locations when we are fortunate enough to plan a vacation. We instinctively know that our soul needs beauty to thrive. We instinctively know that beauty will lift our spirit. Seeking beauty is not frivolous. It is a necessity for living a joyful, peaceful life.

Surrounding our self with beauty once or twice a year is not enough. We need to experience the sacredness of beauty every single day of our life, especially on the rougher ones. When we strip away the unnecessary, we uncover the unnoticed beauty around us. When we consciously simplify, we make room for even more beauty to come into our life. Imagine the difference in your energy when you are able to tap into the sacred beauty in your life every single day because you have created the space for it to be seen.

CHAPTER 10

EMBRACING CONSCIOUS SIMPLICITY

"You cannot hold onto the old all the while declaring that
you want something new. The old will defy the new; the
old will deny the new; the old will decry the new. There is
only one way to bring in the new. You must make room
for it."

~NEALE DONALD WALSH

WE STARTED THIS book with a story about a group of women who
came together one evening to discuss ways to clear clutter and simplify their lives, not fully realizing at the time how it would become
about so much more than the physical clutter. Several weeks after
the initial meeting we scheduled a follow up gathering, thinking
it would be helpful to check in with each other. We also thought
it would be fun to bring some of the items we were releasing that
just might be useful to another woman in the group. The night of
that follow up gathering, Teresa's basement was filled with clothes,
kitchen items, garden tools, jewelry, and home décor no longer
needed by their original owners, but all nice enough to offer up
for the swap. Everyone agreed ahead of time to stay mindful about
taking only what they loved or really needed and that the rest
would be donated the following day. Other than that, there were

no rules and no limits on the number of items one could bring or take home that evening. If it was there, it was up for grabs.

Honestly, Teresa was a bit worried that the little swap might backfire and that some might be tempted to replace all of their old clutter with a new batch of stuff since it was so available, but her concerns proved unwarranted. On the contrary, while everyone did find at least one treasure that night (Teresa will admit to snatching up a gorgeous turquoise scarf), they also managed to stay very mindful of what they were taking. One of the most notable parts of the evening was experiencing how much fun it was for the women to see someone else get excited about something for which they themselves had long since lost excitement. Throw pillows in "just the color I've been looking for," a pair of earrings that "go perfectly with my favorite dress," a brand new crock pot, still in the box that "I've been needing for family gatherings." These were only a few of the items that found new homes where they would actually be enjoyed and put to good use.

At the end of the evening the women gathered upstairs to share their clutter clearing experiences from the previous few weeks. Virtually every woman in the group had a story to tell. In the process of clutter clearing, Marilyn, a single mom on a tight budget, discovered not only an expensive bottle of her favorite perfume and a fair amount of gold jewelry buried in various dresser drawers, but also a significant amount of cash, none of which she remembered stashing away. She was thrilled with her unexpected finds and said she felt like she had hit the lottery. She wondered out loud what other hidden treasures she might be overlooking in her life.

Leigh Ann had been putting off going through a box of her late mother's costume jewelry but decided the time had come to face the task. The jewelry had very little monetary value and much of it was broken or tarnished. Still she struggled with guilt about simply discarding something that her mother had loved so much. But as Leigh Ann described it, what happened when she finally sat down to sort through the box of old clip-on earrings, broaches, and necklaces felt magical to her. While most of the jewelry was not wearable, there were bits and pieces that caught her eye. She found herself salvaging a charm here, a gem stone there until she realized that together those pieces would make a beautiful "memory bracelet." Since jewelry making was one of Leigh Ann's hobbies, she was able to create the bracelet herself and proudly showed it off to the group that evening. In the process of releasing that old jewelry, Leigh Ann stumbled upon a way to honor her Mother's memory that felt really good to her and that also allowed her to release some guilt she had been holding onto.

There were plenty more stories and insights shared that evening with common threads through all of them. The women talked about how clearing out just one room, drawer or cupboard left them wanting to clear more clutter from their homes and from their lives, and almost everyone expressed surprise at having found things they didn't even remember they owned. Many of the women mentioned that understanding the connection between their physical clutter and their state of mind inspired them to become more conscious of what they bring into their homes. Several made connections between physical items they had been holding onto and past relationships they hadn't fully let go. Indeed, stories popped up all around as a new awareness of our non-physical clutter was revealed. Julie, for example, realized how much family drama she had been participating in and how much it had been cluttering up her peace of mind. Having made the decision to no longer listen to, repeat or give energy to the on-going dramas of her extended family, she set her boundaries and felt an immediate sense of relief.

Dallas recognized some of her own inner clutter in the form of resentment she'd been hanging onto toward her employer and vowed to find a way to release it and move her life forward. And then of course there was Linda, whose story we told in Chapter Three and who came to realize that she was cluttering up her present life by hanging onto her anger over the betrayal of a past relationship and her fear of being hurt again. These were just a few of the connections that were made that night and in the weeks that followed.

It would be fair to say that there were unexpected insights along the way for all of us, and that all of us did some growing in the process. While we began with a focus on releasing physical clutter, what became apparent is that physical possessions are just one of the ways we manage to clutter up our life. By allowing our precious time, energy and peace of mind to be taken up with activities, relationships, and thoughts that don't support the life we want or honor who we are, we are doing our self a disservice and holding our self back.

THE ONGOING PROCESS OF CONSCIOUS SIMPLICITY

"Let us reflect on what is truly of value in life, what gives meaning to our lives, and set our priorities on the basis of that."

~ *THE 14TH DALAI LAMA*

One thing the women were in agreement about that evening is that Conscious Simplicity is an on-going process, not a one-time event. We would also add that it's an on-going process of awareness and intention that requires a willingness to look a little deeper at what we allow and keep in our life as well as an understanding of why. It requires having the courage to ask our self some powerful questions. Are we spending our time on the things that matter most to us or are we cluttering it up with activities we no longer participate in or enjoy, responsibilities we've begrudgingly taken on, or relationships that emotionally exhaust us but offer little in return? Are we steering clear of unnecessary drains on our time and energy, or allowing in pointless worry, drama, and gossip? Are we striving to live within our means, or cluttering up our life with unnecessary debt and/or possessions that require more from us than they give? Have we made a conscious effort to forgive or are we holding on to grudges, disappointments, hurts and regrets that serve no useful purpose in our life? Are we making conscious choices in alignment with what we value in our present life, or are we going through life with a lack of awareness of what we are doing. Are we driven by a desire for what fills our spirit and feeds our soul, or are we just trying to fill a void with more stuff?

The more we become culturally conditioned, the more disconnected we can become from our true self. When we become disconnected from our authenticity and ignore our inner hunger for a deeper, more meaningful life, no amount of physical possessions will ever be enough. It's just a matter of time before the excess in our life becomes a burden on our energy and we become overwhelmed and even further disconnected from who we really are. But when we reach for awareness and make conscious choices to put our time, money and energy into the things we value most while releasing the excess, we automatically deepen our relationship with our soul. Life then becomes more meaningful, more enjoyable, and much richer.

Best-selling author and spiritual teacher, Neale Donald Walsh, has suggested asking our self the following question on a regular basis, "Is this really what I came all the way to this planet to experience?" Asking this even as we make the small, day-to-day decisions in life can be an incredibly valuable tool for creating awareness and gauging when our choices, whether large or small, are in alignment with what we value most and when they are not. Cumulatively our daily choices make up our life, whether we are making those choices with awareness or by default. When we make our choices by default, we give away our power. When we make them with awareness, we step into our power to create the life we desire.

Embracing Conscious Simplicity means striving to stay in awareness and intention on a daily basis. It means a willingness to live with authenticity. We all deserve to live a life that is uniquely our own and that we consciously choose for our self. None of us came into this world to live someone else's life. We did not come here to live the life our neighbors appear to be living, the life that society has deemed most desirable, the life the media is trying to sell us, or even the life our parents may have dreamed up for us, unless of course we happen to honestly share that dream. It is our sincere desire that Embracing Conscious Simplicity inspires you to begin making conscious choices that will lead to the life you truly want to live, whatever that may be.

AFTERWORD

"Your life is yours to live, no matter how you choose to live it. When you do not think about how you intend to live it, it lives you. When you occupy it, step into it consciously, you live it."

~GARY ZUKAV

CREATING YOUR VISION

WE INVITE YOU to create your own personal vision for Conscious Simplicity centered upon what matters most to you and what makes your heart sing. Creating your personal vision means you will have a picture of how you want your life to look and feel, based upon your own standards and expectations. As you move forward into your vision, it will help to remember that embracing Conscious Simplicity is not about comparing your life to any other. It's about making your own personal choices and consciously living in alignment with what is most important to you. And it's about stripping away what is not. To help you through the process of creating your vision for Conscious Simplicity, we've provided a guide in the Resources section.

Enjoy the journey to Conscious Simplicity! Embrace it and make it yours!

Resources

Performing an Energy Shifting Ritual

"Smudging" is an ancient tool for shifting the stagnant energy from an object, a room, an entire house or even your body, and for getting the positive energy flowing again. There are many ways to smudge and here we offer one simple method for you to try. While sage bundles are often used in smudging rituals, the method outlined below simply uses sound and intent to shift the energy. Please don't get bogged down with the details. The most important element of smudging is your intent! It is, however, highly recommended that, before smudging, you clean and clear your space of physical clutter.

You will Need:

- Your hands for clapping – or a bell, drum or rattle
- A clear intention for what kind of energy you want to bring into your space.

Steps:

1. Open a window or door (preferably in each room)
2. Set your intention for shifting the energy of your space.

3. Start at your front door and work in a clockwise direction, walking through your home, stating your intention and clapping your hands (or ringing a bell, etc.)

4. Clap, ring, or drum as you walk through your space, covering each corner, doorway, closet, etc. Pay special attention to the corners, because this is where energy tends to get stagnant. Do not forget the basement if you have one.

5. As you move around the house, continue to repeat your intention. If any particular area feels like it needs extra attention, take as much time as you need there. Most likely you will feel a subtle energy shift when it's time to move on.

6. When all rooms have been smudged, simply stop, breathe and state your intention one last time, followed by the words "And so it is!"

7. If you can, leave the windows and/or doors open for another half hour or so to allow the fresh air into your space.

8. Enjoy the positive energy that is now flowing through your space!

CREATING YOUR INTENTION STATEMENT

Connect with the Quiet Place Within: Find a place where you can be alone without disruptions. Turn off your phone and all other electronics. Get comfortable and relax. Allow your mind to let go of the stresses of the day and just be still. Release any expectations or preconceived ideas about what you should or shouldn't want for yourself.

IDENTIFY YOUR "WHY":
Why do I want to embrace Conscious Simplicity? _____

_____

What will I gain from making this choice? _____

What do I want to create more space in my life for? _____

Why is this important to me? _____

What value(s) of mine align with this choice?_____

What need(s) of mine align with this choice? _____

TAKE A LOOK AT WHAT YOU'VE BEEN TELLING YOURSELF:
What limiting thoughts, beliefs and/or old stories do I need to release in order to embrace Conscious Simplicity in my life? _____
_____
_____
_____

CREATE YOUR INTENTION STATEMENT:
Keeping your focus positive and remembering to state what you **do**
want, rather than what you **don't** want, write your statement in the
present tense.
*(Example: "I embrace Conscious Simplicity to create the time and space in
my life to enjoy the things that really matter to me." Or, "I choose to consciously simplify my life so that I have more time and energy to be creative.")*
_____
_____
_____
_____

Statements

SHIFTING INTO THE ENERGY OF GRATITUDE

When we shift our focus to the goodness in our life, we move into the energy of gratitude. When we are in the energy of gratitude, we are able to open our hearts, allow forgiveness in and begin to release both the physical and non-physical clutter we have been holding onto. The following simple "Statements of Gratitude" are designed to help you shift into the energy of gratitude, as you release what no longer serves you.

STATEMENTS OF GRATITUDE

- I recognize and am grateful for all the good in my life.
- I am grateful for the ways this space, this item or this situation has served me so far.
- I am grateful for the opportunity to change the energy of this space.
- I am grateful that someone will find great joy and purposeful use of this item I am now releasing.
- I am grateful for what I have learned and how I have grown in this situation.
- I am grateful that I have the power to simplify my life.

My Additional Statements of Gratitude:

_____

_____

_____

_____

_____

Reaching for Forgiveness

As I prepare to release the clutter energy, what is coming up that I need to forgive? Myself? Another person? A situation? Does it involve unnecessary or wasteful purchases? Procrastination? Not speaking my truth? Not honoring myself? Holding onto the past? Guilt? Shame? Anger? Judgment?

_____

_____

How has my lack of forgiveness kept me from moving forward into the life I now desire?

_____

_____

What story would I need to stop telling myself in order to forgive or to find self-forgiveness? What old thought(s)/belief(s) would I need to release?

_____

_____

What new thought(s)/belief(s) could I choose instead?

_____

_____

What gift(s) have I received from the experience/mistake/situation I am now choosing to forgive? What new understandings/insights, skills and/or strengths have I learned or developed?

_____

_____

How could these gift(s) serve me as I move into creating the life I
now desire?

_____

_____

MY FORGIVENESS "GO TO" STATEMENT

I choose forgiveness. I know it allows me to move my life forward
in wonderful ways. I release old thought patterns and beliefs that
made it difficult to forgive in the past. I focus on gratitude and
all that is good in my life. I recognize the gift(s) that came from
the experience or the person I am now forgiving. I am grateful
for this gift because I know it will serve me well as I create the life
I desire and deserve. I easily and completely release the energy of
the past and any power I have given it.

Shifting Your Perspective with Affirmations

When we **change our perspective** about something, we **change the energy** of it. These affirmations are designed to assist in the process of changing your perspective around any item, space, or situation you may be currently challenged with. Select your favorites or write your own. Remember to keep affirmations in the present tense!

- I consciously set my intention to see "this" differently.
- I release this to support my intention for Conscious Simplicity.
- I choose to create peace and calm in my heart and in my space.
- I am grateful for this opportunity to make room in my life for what's important to me.
- I remember that releasing is a process, not an event.
- I remember to look for peace, rather than perfection and to be kind to myself through this process.
- I remember that I am better able to serve when my life is consciously simplified.
- I remember to stay conscious of what I allow into my home/ space because of the effect it has on my physical, mental and emotional energies.
- I see peace instead of "this". I see and feel peace instead of the distress, disappointment, anger or overwhelm I feel about my space and my stuff.
- I remember to focus on what I am moving toward, rather than what I am moving away from.
- I recognize that this is simply an item rather than the person/ place/event with which I associate it. I can consciously choose to keep the memory without the item.

Helpful Questions for the Release of Clutter Energy

Determine if the Item Fits the Definition of Clutter Energy:

- Does this (item) represent a delayed decision?
- Does this (item) lower my energy?
- Is this (item) without a "home"?
- Has the purpose of this (item) passed?
- Is this (item) broken or in need of repair?
- Am I keeping this (item) "just in case"?
- Is the purpose of this (item) on a "maybe, someday" status?

Determine How Well the Item Currently Serves you:

- Does this (item) serve my vision/intention for this space?
- Does this (item) serve the life I want to live now?
- Is this (item) in alignment with my needs and values?

Additional Questions to Ask when you are Feeling Stuck:

- **How** does this (item) serve my vision/intention?
- **How** does this (item) serve the life I want to live now?
- **How** is this (item) in alignment with my needs and values?
- What thoughts surface when I see this item?
- Do I love it?
- Do I use it?
- Does it lift my spirits when I see it /think about it?

DETERMINE THE STATEMENT THE ITEM MAKES:
What statement would I be making if I choose to keep this?

_____

_____

What statement would I be making if I were willing to release this?

_____

_____

INVISIBLE CLUTTER INVENTORY

EMOTIONAL & MENTAL CLUTTER *Grudges, regrets, guilt, past hurts, expectations, toxic relationships, chronic worrying, old stories, beliefs, approval seeking, negative thoughts or attitudes, complaining, focusing on the past, controlling behavior, over-thinking*	HOW RELEASING THIS WILL SIMPLIFY MY LIFE
COMMUNICATION CLUTTER *Words, noise, gossip, information, e-clutter*	HOW RELEASING THIS WILL SIMPLIFY MY LIFE

ADDITIONAL NON-PHYSICAL CLUTTER *Time, body, drama, financial or spiritual clutter, joyless activities, dishonest behavior, self-denial, multi-tasking*	**HOW RELEASING THIS WILL SIMPLIFY MY LIFE**

CREATING A HEALING SPACE

Here are a few questions to help you imagine your perfect healing space. You may not be able to incorporate everything from your answers into your space, but be creative with the possibilities. For instance, if your ideal healing space would include a view of the ocean, but you live far from the water, consider including photos of the beach, some seashells, or a deep blue blanket in your space. You are aiming for a certain feeling and there are plenty of ways to create the feeling you are after. Just let your imagination run wild.

What would your ideal healing space look like? _____
_____
_____

What would your ideal healing space feel like? _____
_____
_____

What colors, objects, scents, textures/fabrics or elements of nature soothe your soul? _____
_____
_____

How could you incorporate some or all of those into your healing space? _____
_____
_____

What would you insist on including in your healing space? _____
_____
_____

What would you insist on excluding from your healing space? ___
_____
_____

CREATING YOUR VISION FOR CONSCIOUS SIMPLICITY

Begin by identifying the essence of your desire. Although you may not have a full picture of what you want your simplified life to look like, you can identify how you want it to feel. Grab some paper and a pen and write down as many adjectives as you can that describe the life you desire. Do you want a life that is more meaningful? Exciting? Balanced? Abundant? Peaceful? Loving? Drama-free? Soulful? Don't worry if the words you write seem to contradict each other. You are a multi-dimensional being, with many aspects to your personality. There are bound to be some contradictory feelings along the way. Just be honest with yourself. Once you've gained some clarity about how you want your life to feel, you will know the "essence" of your desire.

Imagine for a moment that your life is a blank slate. Just let everything in "life as you know it" go for a moment. The good, the bad, the ugly, and the beautiful, just let it all go. Now, imagine that you have been granted a fresh start; a huge life "do over", but that you must start this "do over" from scratch. The things that are important to you, the people, situations and activities you love, the beliefs you want to hold onto, the parts of life that are in alignment with your heart's desires can be added back later, but for the moment, your life is a blank slate. For now, just let everything go.

Begin to explore the realm of all possibilities. In your mind's eye, begin to fill the blank slate with only the things (possessions, relationships, work, thoughts, behaviors, activities) you love and desire for your life. You will want to makes some notes. Remember this is the realm of all possibilities, so there are no limits to what you can choose. Anything and everything is possible. Just explore and let your heart speak its truth. This is not about what you think you *should* want, or even what you think you can or can't have. You are not committing to anything here. You are just exploring. Nobody is going to force you to make any changes you are not ready to make. Even if your ultimate vision does not feel possible right now, this process will help you gain valuable insight about what is important to you and what you sincerely desire. Just let your imagination create a picture in your mind of a life filled with only what you choose to have in it. Let yourself *feel* into your life of Conscious Simplicity. Imagine how energized, how fulfilled, how peaceful, and how free you will be when you are living a life filled with only what matters most to you. Just sit with that awhile.

Be still and stay open to what comes. Know that there may be some surprises along the way because when we clear away the internal and external clutter in our life, we are in a much better position to hear the whispers of our inner guidance. You may not yet have a full vision for your life of Conscious Simplicity, but hopefully you now at least have a feel for the essence of what you want to create, as well as an idea of what that could look like. Allow your vision to evolve and just enjoy the process. Trust yourself, stay open to all possibilities, be honest with yourself and most of all, choose to have fun with this. Below is a list of helpful questions to help you gain even more clarity.

Helpful Questions for Creating Your Vision

1. What intention have I set for Conscious Simplicity? _____

_____

2. What is the "essence" of my desire for my life? (How do I want my life to feel?) _____

_____

3. What is most important to me in life? _____

_____

4. What do I love? _____

_____

5. What do I value? _____

_____

6. What parts of my current life are in alignment with my deepest held values? _____

_____

7. What parts are not? _____

_____

8. What part(s) of myself do I want to explore and/or express next? _____

_____

9. What inner and outer clutter do I need to let go of in order to move toward the intention I have set for my life? (Ex: beliefs, expectations, activities, grudges, physical possessions, emotional, mental, or time clutter) _____

_____

10. My vision for Conscious Simplicity includes: _____

_____

11. My vision for Conscious Simplicity excludes: _____

_____

12. This is what my life of Conscious Simplicity looks like: _____

_____

13. What is one step I am willing to take toward my vision? _____

_____

Suggested Reading

Clutter and Organizing

Janes, Faith, **Household Simplicity: Practical Minimalism at Work for Your Home,** Faith Janes, 2012

Morgenstern, Julie, **Organizing from the Inside Out,** Henry Holt and Company, LLC, New York, NY, 2004

Nelson, Mike, **Stop Clutter from Stealing Your Life,** Career Press, Franklin Lakes, NJ 2008

Waddill, Kathy, **The Organizing Sourcebook,** McGraw-Hill, New York, NY 10121, 2001

Walsh, Peter, **It's All Too Much,** Free Press, New York NY 2007

Walsh, Peter, **Enough Already,** Free Press, New York, NY 2009

Forgiveness

Casarjian, Robin, **Forgiveness: A Bold Choice for a Peaceful Heart,** Bantam Books, New York, NY 1992

Luskin, Dr. Fred, **Forgive for Good,** HarperCollins, New York, NY 2002

Sacred Spaces and Feng Shui

Griggs Lawrence, Robyn; Coca, Joe, **The Wabi-Sabi House: The Japanese Art of Imperfect Beauty,** 2004

Kingston, Karen, **Clear Your Clutter with Feng Shui,** Broadway Books, New York, 1999

Kingston, Karen, **Creating Sacred Space with Feng Shui,** Karen Kingston, 1996

Linn, Denise, **Feng Shui for the Soul,** Hay House, Inc., Carlsbad, CA, 2000

Linn, Denise, **Sacred Space,** The Random House Publishing Group, New York, 1995

Morrison Meyer, Laurine, **Sacred Home: Creating Shelter for Your Soul,** Llewellyn Publications, St. Paul MN, 2004

SPACE CLEARING
Linn, Denise, **Space Clearing A-Z: How to use Feng Shui to Purify and Bless Your Home,** Hay House, Inc., Carlsbad, CA, 2001

WORKS CITED
Arnold, Jeanne E., Graesch, Anthony P., Ragazzini, Enzo, Ochs, Elinor, Life at Home in the Twenty-First Century: 32 Families Open Their Doors, Cotsen Institute of Archaeology Press, 2012

"Interactions of Top-Down and Bottom-Up Mechanisms in Human Visual Cortex", *The Journal of Neuroscience,* **January 2011, Princeton University Neuroscience Institute**

Made in the USA
San Bernardino, CA
22 April 2016